Open Doors

Open Doors

Western New York African-American Houses of Worship

Edited by

Sharon R. Amos, Ph.D.

and

Sharon A. Savannah

The Writer's Den

Buffalo, New York

Our heartfelt appreciation to those ancestors

who paved the path

and all those who encouraged and supported

our efforts to collect the histories.

Western New York African American Houses of Worship
Leaders, Staff and Members

Florence Hargrave Curtis, Historiographer Western New York
African Methodist Episcopal Conference District 1

EDITORS

Sharon R. Amos Ph.D

Sharon A. Savannah

Layout Assistant and Back Cover Design

Marion Slaughter

Front Cover Design

Archie L. Amos Jr. Graphically Speaking

Photos

Sharon A. Savannah

Houses of Worship Submissions

Word Processing Assistant

Rosetta Savannah

Cover Door Design

Valeria Cray D

Technical Assistant

Jason B. Amos

TABLE OF CONTENTS

INTRODUCTION

A Note from Coeditor Sharon A. Savannah

A Word from the Clergy

A Black Church Experience

HOUSES OF WORSHIP HISTORIES

17INTRODUCTION

Open Doors: Western New York African American Houses of Worship features sixty histories of tabernacles, temples, churches, fellowships, ministries and a mosque. This volume does not purport to be a complete compendium of African American Houses of Worship in Western New York; however, it does provide a representative sampling of predominately African American congregations and African American worship leaders of Baptist, Catholic, Church of God in Christ, Lutheran, Methodist, Pentecostal, non- denominational and other denominational congregations in Buffalo, Lackawanna, Lockport, and Niagara Falls, New York.

In producing this historical volume, we began with the single purpose of collecting church histories for posterity. We found that a number of houses of worship have websites, but there is no central location or source for the many denominations' histories. We emailed, faxed, mailed, and hand delivered requests for the Houses of Worship histories and the deceased clergy biographical sketches.

In return, we were rewarded with the histories that are included in this volume. We have eagerly extracted them from websites, received them from church secretaries, collected them from bulletins and anniversary journals, reconstructed them from clergy obituaries and gleaned them from books and newspapers. Along the way, we expanded our understanding of the sacrifices and determination of many individuals.

In *The Black Church in the African American Experience,* C. Eric Lincoln and Lawrence H. Mamiya identify the "seven major historic black denominations: the African Methodist Episcopal (AME) Church; the African Methodist Episcopal Zion (AMEZ) Church; the Christian Methodist Episcopal (CME) Church; the National Baptist Convention, USA., Incorporated (NBC); the National Baptist Convention of America, Unincorporated (NBCA);

the Progressive National Baptist Convention (PNBC); and the Church of God in Christ (COGIC)," as comprising "the black Church." [1]

However, "two new black denominations have developed: The National Missionary Baptist Convention (NMBC) and the Full Gospel Baptist Church Fellowship (FGBCF). The FGBCF does not refer to itself as a denomination. Yet it is known that blacks were also members of predominantly white denominations such as the Episcopal, Presbyterian, Congregational, United Methodist and Roman Catholic churches. This listing confines 'the black Church,' to "those independent, historic, and totally black controlled denominations, which were founded after the Free African Society of 1787 and which constituted the core of black Christians." [2]

When we take a look at the history of the black church, we find that "by 1789, the black church as a formal institution was established in America, though still in grave danger from those who fought against any assertion of the humanity of Africans or any of their descendants."[3]

In *Preaching with Sacred Fire: An Anthology of African American Sermons, 1750 to the Present,* Delores Williams defines the black church as an "invisible institution."

> The black church is invisible, but we know it when we see it...It has neither hands nor feet nor form, but we know it when we feel it in our communities...It is invisible, but we know when we see, hear and feel it quickening the heart, measuring the soul and bathing

---

[1] C. Eric Lincoln and Lawrence H. Mamiya, *The Black Church in the African American Experience.* (Durham: Duke University Press, 1990) 398

[2] <http://www.blackandchristian.com/blackchurch/>

[3] Martha Simmons and Frank A. Thomas, eds. *Preaching with Sacred Fire: An Anthology of African American Sermons, 1750 to the Present.* (New York: W.W. Norton & Company Inc., 2010) 27.

life with the spirit in time.[4] Whether it's the Holy Spirit in Christian churches, the spirit of beneficence and mercy in Muslim mosques or the ever abiding spirit of the ancestors in African traditional religion,[5] we know it. These early gatherings, secret meetings held in brush arbors, barns, fields and any safe place, of the invisible institution were the religious precursor to black churches.

The invisible institution allowed blacks to establish a cultural identity in a strange land and existed alongside churches blacks attended with whites, churches formed by blacks and for blacks that began with white preachers, and black churches not espousing black liberation.[6]

The church was one of the first community organizations that blacks in Buffalo established in the early 1800's. The congregation that became known as the Michigan Street Baptist Church was formally organized between 1832 and 1837. Bethel African Methodist Episcopal Church evolved from the Colored Methodist Society founded in 1831; in Lockport, the First African Methodist Episcopal Church was deeded land in 1844. By "1927, there were fifteen Negro churches with Negro pastors, all on the black East Side."[7] This collection includes African American Houses of Worship that were founded in the hundred years between the 1830's and 1930's and others that were formed in the following years. We located over 250 listings of African American houses of worship in Western New York. The varied historical accounts of *WNYAAHW* acknowledges small groups that began holding meetings or services in homes and when they outgrew those spaces moved to storefronts and later built or purchased vacant edifices. Some houses of worship

---

[4] Simmons 21.
[5] Simmons xxv.
[6] Simmons 21-22.
[7] Mark Goldman, *High Hopes*. (Albany: SUNY Press 1983)209.

began with a lay worship leader and later invited a minister while others began with an ordained minister.

According to Williams in *Strangers in the Land of Paradise*, "There is evidence that blacks from particular southern cities and/or states organized homogeneous churches based upon geographical origin. Shiloh Baptist, for example, was established in 1916 to accommodate southern born blacks. The minister, Elijah J. Echols, had come to Buffalo from Mississippi and [Burnie McCarley] of St. John Baptist [had come from South Carolina].Their parishioners were also recent migrants who often were repulsed by the formality of the established churches in the black community and the aloofness of their members."[8] The majority of the birthplaces of the deceased clergy included in this volume are South Carolina, Alabama, Mississippi, and Arkansas.

We discovered many interesting facts along the way. Buffalo's houses of worship have served as hosts to Booker T. Washington, Reverend Martin Luther King, Malcolm X and other notable figures.

Although Buffalo does not have megachurches (2000 members attending weekly) like many larger cities, we found that here some ministers serve as pastor for more than one church or they are the pastor of multiple locations: Bishop Troy A. Bronner, Pastor Roderick L. Hennings, the late Pastor Major Jenkins,[9] Pastor Darius Pridgen, and Pastor John H. Williams.

No longer are African American houses of worship all on the eastside of Buffalo. They are located in nearly every section of

---

[8] Lillian Serece Williams. *Strangers in the Land of Paradise*. (Bloomington: Indiana University Press, 1999) 63.
[9] Nick Salvatore. *Singing in a Strange Land: C.L. Franklin, the Black Church, and the Transformation of America* (New York: Little and Brown Company 2006)79. Reverend Jenkins pastored Friendship in Buffalo and Greater White Stone in Memphis, TN in the 1930's.

the city with several African American Houses of Worship in the suburbs: in 2005, Zion Dominion moved to Amherst; Good Samaritan Church of God in Christ moved to Cheektowaga in 2010 and New Cedar Grove followed in 2011. According to Mount Olive's history, it began in Tonawanda and later moved to Buffalo.

Worship leaders who served were sometimes related: the Reverends Echols, father and son, both pastored First Shiloh; the Reverends S.K. Lewis and John Williams, two brothers, pastored New Zion; and the Reverends Henry Ford, Glenn DuBois, and C.C. Cox, the three pastors of Jordan Grove, have all been brothers-in-law.

Seeking locations that served the needs of the membership, often houses of worship relocated numerous times. A number of current African American congregations worship in former Lutheran, Episcopal and Evangelical church buildings. Often members of those original congregations moved to the suburbs as the neighborhoods' demographics changed, i.e. grew increasingly diverse. One Niagara Falls architect, Wallace V. Moll, has designed edifices for African American congregations that include Cold Spring Church of God in Christ, Evening Star Church of God in Christ, First Calvary Missionary Baptist Church, Mount Zion Baptist Church in Niagara Falls, New York; New Zion Institutional Missionary Baptist Church, Pleasant Grove Baptist Church, St. John Baptist Church, and Zion Missionary Baptist Church.[10] Also, a skilled African American brick mason, Ray Black, worked on the construction and renovation of many local African American houses of worship.

---

[10] James Napora,."Houses of Worship: A Guide to the Religious Architecture of Buffalo, New York" <http://www.buffaloah.com>

A number of houses of worship in this volume have already held centennial celebrations: Bethel African Methodist Episcopal Church(180), First African Methodist Episcopal Church Lockport, Humboldt Parkway Baptist Church and the Michigan Avenue Baptist Church, and St. Philips Episcopal Church (150); St. John A.M.E. Church (105) is acclaimed as the first black church in Niagara Falls. Within the next decade, others will reach the 100 year hallmark

The last section of *Open Doors* includes brief biographical sketches of deceased worship leaders who served in the Western New York houses of worship. "We Speak Your Names: A Tribute to Deceased Clergy" highlights their callings and their work in the African American and the ecumenical community. We also note that a few of the deceased clergy were born in the 19th century; the majority of the clergy were born in the southern states, and many served in the military.

In conclusion, we recognize the historic challenges as well as the current challenges of African American Houses of Worship.

> Black Churches are not perfect institutions but with all their limitations they represent the institutionalized staying power of the human community that has been under siege for close to 400 years. Black personalities, movements, and ideologies have waxed and waned over the years and will continue to do so, but black churches have remained a firm anchor stabilizing the black experience in giving it meaning through the uncertain eras of change and counter change. The black church is, after all, no more and no less than the black people who comprise it and it mirrors the imagination, the interest, and the sense of urgency of the black community it serves and symbolizes.[11]

---

[11] C. Eric Lincoln and Lawrence H. Mamiya

We invite our readers to enter through the Open Doors of Western New York African American Houses of Worship, celebrate our diverse religious community, and learn about its history.

Sharon R. Amos PhD., Editor

NOTE: *SOME HOUSES OF WORSHIP LEADERS MAY HAVE CHANGED.*

A Note from Sharon A. Savannah, Editor

While researching the histories of the various African American churches for WNYAAHW, I became more and more intrigued with their diverse heritage. This experience has been more than enlightening, it has been adventurous. And what an adventure it has turned out to be.

Sharon Amos and I started our search by using Google to identify the many church conferences so we could then obtain listings of the various churches and houses of worship. This in itself turned out to be eye-opening not just because of the large number of denominations and faiths, but also because of the similarities in names which crossed those boundaries. Several listings we found under different categories that often identified one entity and just as often pointed to another one altogether.

After finding approximately 250 initial listings, I decided to ride around Buffalo and see how close to the number we were. Was I surprised to see that there were actually more than we had calculated! We decided to start with the list and we proceeded to send out letters requesting histories from these houses of worship. Not addressing the letter to a specific individual turned out to be a bit of an issue. I thought that, as in my home church, there is usually one person designated to open mail and direct it to the appropriate person. Well, this proved not to be the case in a lot of churches and some letters went unread even after we sent at least two more. We then decided that the next best thing to do would be to make personal calls to the worship houses. Again, this was a challenge. We found many churches have made cutbacks, so many offices are no longer manned by the church secretary ready to take information and tell us when the pastor will be in. We heard answering machines with intricate voice commands on what number to press to leave messages. If we did get someone, usually the answer was one of no recollection of having received the original request but could we fax another or e-mail the information. Sometimes we actually spoke to the Pastor who would then promise he would send us the information or contact the person who was designated to handle such requests. On some occasions, we would be referred to his wife whom he would ask to handle the matter. These methods resulted in some responses.

Our next idea was to go on a journey and make personal requests for this information. We had been in contact with a church secretary who was extremely helpful in identifying some of the African American houses of worship in Niagara Falls. After making a list of the locations we were given, we set out on our journey one Sunday morning in 2010. We pulled up the GPS on our cell phones and headed out to churches in neighboring Niagara Falls and Lackawanna. We were met with yet another challenge. The first things we learned--do not rely on cell phone mapping being correct and that with construction roadways may not be in the same places they once were! Getting to Niagara Falls was easy, getting around Niagara Falls-- that was a different story. Neither of us being familiar with the area, we got to the city and began to look around for signs to determine what direction we should go in. Checking our mapping, we soon realized that the street we thought we should be had ended at a new plaza. Now we had to rely on our sense of direction and intuition. After locating the churches in Niagara Falls, we realized that we had actually made it to about twelve of them, all either before services were over or just as they were ending.

After we had compiled several histories through research and responses, with a little bit of nagging, I decided to start getting pictures of some of these edifices. I began taking a few, and then we decided to venture out together once again. This journey was a little more direct in its purpose as we had decided we needed to start finalizing what would become this book. Two of the histories were for churches located in Lockport, NY. As this was the furthest away for us, we went there first planning to go to Niagara Falls on our way back to Buffalo. Having done photography in association with my previous employment, I was ready. With digital photography being so popular nowadays, most photographers no longer use 35mm film. But I still love my "old school" camera with the different lenses and I can get the most out of it. Knowing I wanted to show each church in the best possible light, I hurriedly loaded my camera and began to take photos. We were very proud that we had found the churches in Lockport with no problems, and with some ease we arrived in Niagara Falls and began taking the photos there. After about the second church, I realized that in my haste I had not advanced the film when I closed the back of the camera, so, of course, I had captured nothing. We headed back to Lockport to retake photos.

Despite the many ups and downs and snafus we are finally here presenting our book of African American Houses of Worship. Just to see and read about these houses of worship and their founders was insightful for me. After becoming aware of the great number of African American houses of worship, I began to see and feel just how much prominence religion holds in the life of the community. As I journeyed throughout the area taking pictures, I noticed that the pride and essence of the worship is shown not only in the words but also in the structures: from store fronts to grand old edifices to gleaming new buildings. Churches use pictures and murals and gardens to enhance their surroundings that give evidence of how much the place they worship means to them. I hope to expand this project further by getting more churches to document and archive their history no matter how long or short it may be. This portion of the African American legacy must be maintained and passed on from generation to generation.

May our history with its blessings and struggles never be forgotten.

A Black Church Experience

In a speech in Philadelphia, Pennsylvania in 2008, former Senator Barack Obama now President Barack Obama felt it was necessary to defend his church, Trinity United Church of Christ in Chicago. In [his] first book, *Dreams From My Father*, [he] described the experience of [his] first service at Trinity:

> People began to shout, to rise from their seats and clap and cry out, a forceful wind carrying the reverend's voice up into the rafters....And in that single note - hope! - I heard something else; at the foot of that cross, inside the thousands of churches across the city, I imagined the stories of ordinary black people merging with the stories of David and Goliath, Moses and Pharaoh, the Christians in the lion's den, Ezekiel's field of dry bones. Those stories - of survival, and freedom, and hope - became our story, my story; the blood that had spilled was our blood, the tears our tears; until this black church, on this bright day, seemed once more a vessel carrying the story of a people into future generations and into a larger world. Our trials and triumphs became at once unique and universal, black and more than black; in chronicling our journey, the stories and songs gave us a means to reclaim memories that we didn't need to feel shame about...memories that all people might study and cherish - and with which we could start to rebuild.

That has been my experience at Trinity. Like other predominantly black churches across the country, Trinity [United Church of Christ] embodies the black community in its entirety - the doctor and the welfare mom, the model student and the former gang-banger. Like other black churches, Trinity's services are full of raucous laughter and sometimes bawdy humor. They are full of dancing, clapping, screaming and shouting that may seem jarring to the untrained ear. The church contains in full the kindness and cruelty, the fierce intelligence and the shocking ignorance, the struggles and successes, the love and yes, the bitterness and bias that make up the black experience in America.[12]

---

[12] "A More Perfect Union", Philadelphia,PA, March 18, 2008.
<http://my.barackobama.com/page/content/hisownwords>

Sunday morning ritual

On Sunday mornings we come together early

Disregarding the raiment of the week

Those worn garments of lived out realities,

Outlived fantasies and prayer

We come together early...[13]

-Imani Constace Johnson Burnett

---

[13] Gloria Wade-Gayles ed. *My Soul is a Witness.Boston:Beacon Press,1995*

A Word from the Clergy

Reverend Dr. Ivery Daniels
Pastor of White Rock Missionary Baptist Church

There is a need for all people of faith that believe in justice to work together for the common good. We need to end hunger and homelessness in a country that has so much. While many of us are Christians, those that are not differ in doctrine and teachings. The work of saving souls and preaching the Word that I set out to do as a pastor/minister nearly 45 years ago has not changed, while other things have. Many local churches have been impacted by the growing numbers of members who have relocated to the South for jobs or family, by the growing number of retirees, by the distractions away from church like the Sunday sale of alcohol, by the growing legal and illegal drug abuse, and by extended mall shopping hours. Many members and their families who had one car or who walked to church regularly attended services. Now many families have two or three cars. In some instances, early morning services at 7:00 or 8:00 a.m. give church members more time to go other places and do other non-church things. Today young people have more opportunities to do work in the church. They don't have to wait until they are old. We all need to know the history of our struggles, but especially young people need to know the sacrifices that have been made in their behalf. The civil rights movement was based in the black church. The church is relevant today. More workers are needed in the vineyards.

The doors are open. You are welcome to join us.

Agape African Methodist Episcopal Church
222 Northland Avenue
Buffalo, New York

The Agape Church of Divine Love (known as Agape African Methodist Episcopal Church) was organized on September 14, 1969 in the home of Mr. and Mrs. Edward Stenhouse. During the early months of the church's existence, services were held in the homes of various members, the Michigan Avenue YMCA, and the Lutheran Church of the Redeemer. The persons forming this independent congregation had previously been members of the Delaine Waring AME Church of Buffalo, New York.

Founding members were the late Reverend Melvin Crawford, Sister Eldera Goldsmith, Pedro A. Castro, Clara Mae Castro, Angelina Castro, Diodi Castro, Charles E. Kelley, Emma Louise Kelley, Rhonda Kelley, Bonita Kelley, Kerwin Kelley, April Kelley, Deborah Casper, Patricia Kelley, Marguerite Mitchell, Thelma Phelps, Thelma Stenhouse, Barbara Patton, James Patton, Coralyn Patton, Kelley Patton, Betty Walker, Toni Walker, Bessie Scott, Ickey Mae Williamson, Alex Williamson, Lovell Williamson, Edna Shaw, Michael Shaw, Lamont Shaw, Richard Shaw, Bruce Shaw, and Linda Shaw. Under Reverend Whitfield Washington's leadership, 1970 – 1973, the congregation was granted permission to use the former sanctuary of the Lutheran Evangelical Church of the Atonement located at 222-224 Northland Avenue, Buffalo, New York.

The entire church was leased to the Build Unity Independence Liberty and Dignity Organization (B.U.I.L.D.) by the Lutheran Co-Ordinate Ministry of Buffalo. The church also obtained its charter as a religious institution.

The Agape Church of Divine Love voted to seek admission to the New York Annual Conference of the A.M.E. Church through the encouragement of Reverend Charles Smith, an interim pastor for six months in 1973, and Reverend Floyd N. Black, interim pastor six months in 1973-1974. The church's name was changed to Agape African Methodist Episcopal Church.

The late Bishop Ernest L. Hickman assigned the Reverend Theodore Hudson 1974 -1977 as pastor. Under Reverend Hudson's leadership, his wife, Joyce served as one of the church musicians. A parsonage was purchased at 1008 Humboldt Parkway.

Bishop Richard Allen Hildebrand assigned the Reverend A. Frederick A. Lucas, 1977-1982, as pastor. Under the leadership of Reverend Lucas, negotiations began with the Lutheran Co-Ordinate Ministry of Buffalo to purchase the entire 222-224 Northland Avenue property. On Sunday, February 17, 1980, Bishop Hildebrand presented a check in the amount of $60,000.00 for the purchase of the Lutheran Evangelical Church of the Atonement. These funds were raised in a phenomenal nineteen months with the assistance of the First Episcopal District and the Connectional church. Agape now possessed the land. On June 11, 1980, M&T Bank granted the congregation a $100,000.00 mortgage for the purpose of renovating the church structure.

Ministers uniting with Agape and persons answering the call to preach were Reverend Robert Locke, Reverend Milton Hammett, Reverend Samuel King, Richard Stenhouse, Barbara Austin-Lucas, Thomas Davis Jr., Virgil Hammett, Harvey Hammett, Anthony Pinn, Anne Hargrave-Pinn, Janet Jenkins,

Gerald Hesson, Gwendolyn Collins, Ada Albert, Mary Graham, James Fears, and Robin Franklin.

Bishop Richard Allen Hildebrand assigned the Reverend Dr. Andrew T. Holtz Jr., 1982-1986 as pastor. Under Reverend Holtz's leadership, the 8:00am worship service, the food pantry, the soup kitchen, Chapel Hour, and the Agape Crisis Intervention Center were instituted. "Sisters Sharing" the theme of a weekend retreat held at the Buffalo Hilton Hotel. It was organized by Reverend Barbara A. Lucas as part of a missionary endeavor, and over 1000 women from the United States, Canada and Bermuda attended.
This initiative was scheduled prior to Reverend Holtz's assignment to Agape. Persons answering the call to preach were Lenora Fears, Derrick Harris, Ruth Harris, Elreda Hollingsworth, and E.J. Robinson. Bishop Frank C. Cummings assigned the Reverend Robert O. Bailey 1986-1988 as pastor.
Under Reverend Robert O. Bailey's leadership, the congregation liquidated its outstanding debts and purchased additional properties. A parsonage was purchased at 37 Blaine Avenue. The majority of the renovations were done by Reverend Bailey. Answering the call to preach was Burnie J. Savage who entered as a local minister.

Bishop Frank C. Cummings assigned Reverend James E.F. Lawrence (1988-1992) as pastor. Under Reverend James E.F. Lawrence's leadership, the Annual Gourmet Gents Affair (a food tasting event featuring men who cook) was begun. The Missionary Society dedicated the naming of its society: The Annie W. Hargrave Missionary Society. Kenyatta Cobb answered the call to preach.

Bishop Frank C. Cummings assigned Reverend Wayne A. Johnson Sr., (1992- 2001) as pastor. Under Reverend Johnson's leadership, several improvements and upgrades were made. Glass block windows adorned the Fellowship Hall featuring the center windows with three crosses, and glass block windows were installed in the ladies and men's rest rooms and

Young /Children's Division classroom. A baby grand piano was a gift to Agape from Pastor Johnson in memory of his father, Elder Arthur N. Johnson. New carpet was installed in the educational wing and the second floor offices. An outside church directory was donated by H. Alfred Lewis Mortuary along with a new boiler.

The finance office was dedicated in memory of our founding members, Sister Bessie Scott and Brother Charles Kelley. David Hill answered the call to preach.

Bishop Donald G.K. Ming assigned Reverend Dr. Natalie P. Alford (2001-2004) as pastor. Under Reverend Alford's leadership, a Women's Ministry and a tape ministry were established. Reverend Alford is Agape's first female pastor.

Bishop Richard F. Norris assigned Reverend Horace T. Cromer (2004-2009) as pastor. Under Reverend Cromer's leadership, the administrative offices were upgraded. Bishop Richard F. Norris assigned Reverend William Cobb Sr., 2009-2010 as pastor.

Reverend Stenhouse 2010-2011 served as interim pastor. Under his leadership, Agape paid the church mortgage loan in 30 days. The mortgage holder agreed to forgive the balance. Restorations were made to the parsonage.

Bishop Richard F. Norris assigned Reverend Brandon Karl Allen on February 12, 2011, as pastor at the Founder's Day Celebration.

From *Taking the Old Path and Preserving Our Legacy*, compiled by Florence Hargrave Curtis, Western New York African Methodist Episcopal Conference District 1, Historiographer; 2011 Updates provided by Terry Patterson

Antioch Baptist Church
1327 Fillmore Avenue
Buffalo, New York

The organization of the Antioch Baptist Church began with a vision by Reverend J.N. Robinson in 1929. On September 17, 1931, a small group of people met in the home of Reverend Robinson at 248 Purdy Street, Buffalo, New York. Each week the group, called the Prayer Band, met for prayer services and by 1932 it had outgrown the apartment. A small church had formed. Reverend Robinson financed and worked diligently restoring a rundown house at 264 Purdy Street. Upon completion of the building, a small but beautiful place of worship had formed. On the second Sunday

in May 1932, the Prayer Band moved into its new church home and began having Sunday school and church services.

On November 20, 1932, the church was organized and Reverend Robinson named it the Antioch Baptist Church. The guest speaker for the dedicatory service was Reverend L.A. Holloway of the Union Baptist Church. Other ministers present were Reverend W. Harris and Reverend E.J. Echols of Shiloh Baptist Church. In 1935, Antioch purchased the building at 262 Purdy Street. On March 27, 1939 the certificate of organization was acknowledged. On April 18, 1939 at 4:11p.m., the certificate was stamped by the Erie County Clerk's Office.

With God's blessings, four years later in 1943, the mortgage was paid in full. Antioch's only elected assistant pastor was Reverend Pitts, and Mother Alberta White was the first member to be baptized during the 30's. Other members during the organizing period were Mother Jesse Toney, Mr. Leroy Edwards, Deacon Temer, Mr. George Barton, Mr. Lucious Copeland, Rose Carson and Doris Bowens.

Under the leadership of Reverend Robinson, the first auxiliaries to be organized were Sunday school, Missionary, Pastor's Aide, Willing Workers, Usher Board, Gospel Chorus, BYPU and he began the Building Fund. The facilities at 264 Purdy Street became inadequate, making it necessary to purchase a larger building. Some of the loyal members mortgaged their homes and others contributed cash towards the purchase of 127-131 Florida Street. In 1956, the congregation moved into its new church home at 131 Florida Street.

The parsonage was located at 127 Florida Street. Reverend Robinson worked faithfully until illness obstructed his ability to serve. Reverend O.C. Taylor presided over the pulpit during Reverend Robinson's illness.

In 1961, due to the prolonged illness of Reverend Robinson, Reverend Guy J. Graves was elected and installed as Pastor of the Antioch Baptist Church. Under Reverend Grave's leadership, funds were set aside to pay the rent and some of the living expenses for Reverend and Mrs. Robinson until the death of each of them. Many improvements were made under the leadership of Reverend Graves. A new church parsonage was purchased at 68 N. Parade Street. The pulpit furniture purchased at this time is currently in the pulpit today.

In 1964, members heard the great news that a new broadcast station was in the making and would be featuring religious and church programs. Sister Emma Terry and others were granted permission by Pastor Graves to start fundraising, so that the

Antioch Baptist church would be able to be featured on the new station.

In 1965, Antioch Baptist Church became one of the first churches to be aired on WBLK-FM. Over forty five years later, Antioch is still being aired on WBLK.

In February 1976, Reverend Graves was relieved of his pastoral duties at the Antioch Baptist Church. Reverend Columbus Perkins presided over the pulpit during the absence of a pastor. In March 1976, the deacons and trustees called a meeting for the reorganization and overview of the financial obligations of the church in the absence of a pastor. In April 1976, a meeting was called and the Deacons reported that they were in the process of seeking a pastor. The Trustees were given authorization to obtain information from an architect for building a new church.

At a later meeting, information from the architect revealed that it was not feasible to build a church at this time, and Mr. Conyers and the Trustee Board were given authorization to search for an existing building.

During a later meeting, the Trustees presented information on the possibility of purchasing 1327 Fillmore Avenue and were delegated to proceed with negotiations. It was suggested and accepted that Antioch would wait until a pastor was elected before any purchase of property was finalized.

In November 1976, Reverend William A. Bunton Jr. was elected and installed as Pastor of the Antioch Baptist Church. The following year, under the leadership of Reverend Bunton, the purchase of properties at 1631-1640 Jefferson Avenue and 158 Northland Street were finalized. On November 13, 1978, the purchase of 1327 Fillmore Avenue, the present home of the Antioch Baptist Church, was finalized for the sum of $45,000 cash.

Under the leadership of Reverend Bunton, numerous improvements have been made and continue to take place. Bible classes, Angel Choir, television, radio, tape ministry, prayer line, J.N. Robinson Scholarship Fund, Dr. Watts Choir, food pantry, van service, youth ushers were organized. The Antioch Male Chorus was reorganized along with the expansion of the Sunday school department, vacation bible school, community outreach, and the after school program.

Antioch is currently an active member of The National Baptist Congress of Christian Education, USA Inc., and the Western New York Great Lakes Association. Presently, we continue to move forward in our plans to erect the William A. Bunton Family Life Center. May God continue to bless our church family.

Submitted by Antioch Baptist Church

Bethel African Methodist Episcopal Church
1525 Michigan Avenue
Buffalo, New York

When the Colored Methodist Society of Buffalo was founded in 1831, the Afro-American population of Buffalo numbered approximately 300 persons. The meeting which resulted in the formation of the Colored Methodist Society was held initially in a frame house on Carroll Street. During the first several years of its existence, this society had no official ties with the African Methodist Episcopalian denomination.

The Reverend Richard Williams, one of the earliest A.M.E. itinerant ministers, was the first regularly ordained and accredited elder who carried the banner of the African Methodists of the Episcopal Church and planted them on the shores of Canada and Western New York.

When the New York Annual Conference convened on June 10, 1837, that body accepted and considered petitions from "St. Catherine's Canada West and from Buffalo asking for pastoral care." The New York Conference passed resolutions to send missionaries "into Canada and the western part of the state of New York, to explore, and as far as possible, organize and regulate what society's make they can in these regions."

Bishop Daniel Payne summarized the proceedings of the New York conference in 1838: Reverend Richard Williams had established a society at Rochester, consisting of 26 persons, and also licensed a local preacher to watch over their spiritual interests. He also planted one church at Buffalo with 31 members and licensed two local preachers. "Brother George Weir, Sr., was ordained a deacon to serve the Buffalo Society."

Reverend George Weir, Sr., the first A.M.E. teacher pastor assigned to the "Colored Methodist" Church of Buffalo, was described as a mulatto, and he served the congregation and community for about ten years.

The Census tracts of 1850 indicate that the Weir family came to Buffalo from North Carolina. Under Reverend Weir, the congregation moved from Carroll Street to a frame building on Vine Street in 1839 (the former Vine Street is now the block of William Street that lies between Oak and Elm Streets). In 1845, the frame building on Vine Street was replaced with the new brick structure at a cost of $3000. During his tenure in Buffalo, Reverend Weir was actively involved in efforts to improve the economic, social, and political conditions of his people. His activities were frequently reported in contemporary Afro-American newspapers, the *Colored American* and the *North Star*. In 1847, Reverend Weir was succeeded as pastor by the Reverend Thomas W. Jackson who served the church for one year.

In 1848, the New York A.M.E. Conference sent Reverend Charles Burch to the Vine Street congregation. It was during Reverend Burch's two-year tenure that many of the leading officers and members of the Vine Street congregation left the church and organized what was called the East Presbyterian Church. The dissenters included Richard Jones, a whitewasher; and Richard Turner, a cook; they were two of the more affluent members of Buffalo Afro-American community. George Weir Jr. was also among those who left the Vine Street congregation, and all of those mentioned became officers in the newly formed church.

The New York A.M.E. Conference attempted to reverse its losses in Western New York by sending one of its top young ministers to the Vine Street Church in1850. Reverend Jabez P. Campbell became pastor of the Buffalo station and he immediately set out to affect the revival of the work of God among the members of the churches of Western New York. Two years later, at the New York A.M.E. Conference, Reverend Henry J. Johnson was appointed to the Buffalo station. He arrived on July 27, 1854. Several months after his arrival, the Sabbath school was improving and the congregation had established a library for the use of the schoolchildren. It appears Reverend Johnson spent only one year at the Vine Street Church. He was succeeded by Reverend James M. Williams and Leonard Patterson, each of whom spent one year at the Vine Street Church. In 1857, the Dred Scott decision was pronounced by the Supreme Court and some believed it marked the eve of the Civil War. From 1857-1859, Reverend Deaton Dorrell served the Vine Street Church congregation and he returned to Buffalo for two additional years in 1862. Reverend Dorrell's skills as preacher, manager, and administrator were well-used in Buffalo.

The years between 1831 and 1860 were crucial years in the history of the Vine Street Church. In addition to struggling to maintain itself as an organization it was also forced by circumstance to provide a multitude of services to an Afro-American community that had to rely almost solely on the church to unravel its day-to-day problems. In the three decades prior to the Civil War most American Protestant churches in the northern states were directly involved in the American reform movement.

In Buffalo, New York, the Vine Street A.M.E. Church, the Michigan Street Baptist Church carried the reform movement to the cities and the Afro-American community. The American reform movement was a religious movement aimed at eliminating sin and immorality from the fabric of national life. The movement launched a direct attack on slavery, alcoholic beverages, gambling, war and many other unchristian practices. A major thrust of the reform movement among northern blacks was aimed at improving the overall status of people of color. During the pre-Civil War years, the pastors and congregations of the Vine Street A.M.E. Church laid a solid foundation on which future generations could build.

While the nation, the general A.M.E. church, and the city of Buffalo enjoyed tremendous growth and expansion in terms of its population and its finances during the post-Civil War era, the Vine Street A.M.E. Church of Buffalo and the Afro-American population of the city remained close to its pre-Civil War level. In 1865, the founding of St. Philip's Episcopal Church caused a three-way split in the churchgoing population of this small African-American community. St. Philip's continued to grow and by 1890 it reported the largest ecclesiastical racial group in Buffalo.

The Vine Street Church was served by a number of gifted and exceptional ministers during those post-Civil War years, but the church as a whole did not appear to be moving forward. The Emancipation Proclamation became effective in January 1863. Jubilee celebrations in southern and northern communities were held by the colored people of Buffalo who set apart January 28, 1863 as a day to celebrate this grand event at the Vine Street Church. The exercises of the day commenced with religious services at 10 am and the sermon was preached by Elder Deaton Dorrell.

In 1864, the New York Conference sent the Reverend Francis J. Peck to pastor the Vine Street Church. Reverend Peck, at age 18, began preaching in his father's church. In 1863 at age 29, the young preacher enrolled at Wilberforce where he remained for one year, but a lack of funds ended his stay. He applied to Bishop Daniel Payne for pastoral work and was sent to the New York Conference and subsequently assigned to the Buffalo station. Reverend Peck enjoyed two years of popularity with the Buffalo church. His replacement was the Reverend W.T. Catto, a newly ordained minister who had previously been associated with the Presbyterian Church.

In 1868, the Reverend Elisha Weaver was one of the many talented and educated ministers sent to the Vine Street Church. He spent one year leading the Vine Street A.M.E. Church family. The 1870s brought Reverend Abraham C. Crippen who served two nonconsecutive terms; Reverend J. W. Cooper and Reverend J. G. Mowbray each served Vine Street for two years, and for one year the Reverend Caleb Woodyard pastored the church. In 1879, Vine Street AME Church was renamed First A.M.E. Church with Reverend George C. Bailey as pastor.

In 1912, Reverend A. C. Sanders renamed the First A.M.E. Church, Bethel A.M.E. Church. In the 1920s, Vine Street bought and demolished Bethel Lutheran Church at 551 Eagle Street in order to widen its parameters.

The 1920s and 40s witnessed great growth because of black migration from the South. In the 50s, urban development and redevelopment programs caused Bethel to seek a new home. Under the leadership of Reverend Harry White Sr., Bethel relocated to its current home at 1525 Michigan Avenue in 1953. Formerly Covenant Presbyterian Church, it was purchased for $120,000. With the Reverend White's ability to raise and manage large sums of money effectively the church was virtually debt-free by 1962.

Call it Carroll Street, Vine Street, or Bethel A.M.E. Church, this church was not born before its time. In its long and illustrious history a multitude of pastors (approximately 55) have been assigned to lead the congregation, beginning with Reverend Weir in 1836 and leading up to the current pastor, Reverend Richard Stenhouse.

From *Taking the Old Path and Preserving Our Legacy*, compiled by Florence Hargrave Curtis, Western New York African Methodist Episcopal Conference District 1, Historiographer

Bethel African Methodist Episcopal Church
443 Steelawanna Avenue
Lackawanna, New York

Bethel African Methodist Episcopal Church was organized in 1923 at 443 Steelawanna Avenue in Lackawanna, New York, under the leadership of the Reverend S.S. Williams. The charter members were Joseph Shoffner, William Shoffner, Edward Gimbel, Joseph Smith, Marcel Broom, Marcel Miller, Alice Crawford, Arlene Hawkins, Luther Clapp, Mr. and Mrs. Richard Alexander, the Levi Hawkins family and the Green family. After six years, the congregation acquired a building on Wasson Avenue in Lackawanna. During the Depression, Bethel established a soup kitchen which fed more than 200 people daily.

For a decade and a half, many pastors served the Bethel congregation. Among them were the Reverends Delima, Sterling, Allene, McClendon, Broomes, Daniel Turk, and Thompson. Under the leadership of Reverend Thompson, the church disbanded.

In 1948, the Right Reverend Douglas Ormond B. Walker, pastor of Bethel A.M.E. Church of Buffalo, was consecrated as the 66th Bishop of the African Methodist Episcopal Church. Bishop Walker arranged a meeting with the former members of Bethel Lackawanna and the church was reorganized. The Reverend George Smith was appointed to serve as pastor of the reorganized church. He served the congregation for twenty years.

The Reverend T.J. Woodyard, then pastor of the Ebenezer Baptist Church, assisted Reverend Smith and the congregation with building a sanctuary at 11 Lohr Street on land owned by Joseph Shoffner, a charter member.

The congregation began to grow and these names were added to the rolls: Mrs. Sally Smith, Mrs. Carrrie B. Lee, Mr. and Mrs. James Young and family, Albert and Aurelia Troxler, Emma Wilson, Emma Graham, Mar Johnson, Mrs. Rose Gripper and family, Mrs. Ludy and Mrs. Kennedy. During this time Bethel established strong roots in the Lackawanna community.
The church adopted the name "Baby Bethel" after Bethel in Buffalo, and was again named Bethel A.M.E. Church.
Following Reverend Smith's service, the Reverend Henry Lewis, Sr. served Bethel for a short while.

In 1981, Bishop Richard Allen Hildebrand, presiding prelate of the first Episcopal District appointed Reverend Clara Castro to serve as pastor of Bethel A.M.E. Church. Under the leadership of Reverend Castro, the church was incorporated into the African Methodist Episcopal Church on October 26, 1981.

In May 1982, the Reverend Richard Alan Stenhouse was appointed pastor of Bethel. In June 1982, the congregation purchased the old Ebenezer Baptist Church building located at 21 Steelawanna Avenue. The building was renovated under the direction of Reverend Stenhouse. The following members were instrumental in this renovation: Leroy Giles, Joseph Shoffner, Albert Troxler, Larry Giles, Ashberry Jerad, James Young, Nolan Thomas, Frank Thomas, David Billingsley, Barbara

Anderson, Vivian Thomas, Laura Brown, and Hazel and Jared Buckner. The work was completed on April 10, 1983.

On October 15, the congregation marched into the sanctuary using the theme song *We are Marching to Zion*. Bishop Richard Allen Hildebrand presided over the dedication service. Also participating in the service were Presiding Elder Vernon I. Lowe, Pastor Richard Alan Stenhouse, Reverends Floyd Black, Earl Johnson, Eugene McAshen, Henry Lewis, Fred A. Lucas Jr., and Clara Castro.

From 1984-1992 under the leadership of Bishop Frank C. Cummings, the following pastors were appointed to serve Bethel A.M.E. Church of Lackawanna: The Reverends David Boston, Sylvester Beeman, Carleton Gibson, Darryl Ashford, and Elijah Green.

During the administration of Presiding Prelate Bishop Philip R. Cousin, the Western New York Annual Conference was born in 1996. At this time, the Reverend James Hill Jr. was appointed to serve Bethel Lackawanna. Bishop Cousin appointed the Reverend Natalie P. Alford as pastor during Western New York's second Annual Conference. During her tenure, Reverend Alford focused on spiritual healing, prayer, growth, and financial stewardship.

On October 17, 1998, Bishop Cousin appointed the Reverend William Cobb as under shepherd to the Bethel Lackawanna congregation. Reverend Cobb's emphasis during his seven year tenure was on the word of God, spiritual revival, unity, the power of prayer, and the reorganization and building of the church structure.

Under his leadership and with the encouragement of the current administration of the first Episcopal District under the leadership of Presiding Prelate Bishop Richard Franklyn Norris; Mother Mary Norris, Episcopal Supervisor; and Presiding Elder Reverend James E. F. Lawrence, Bethel Lackawanna pledged to be faithful and loyal stewards to its community, its Conference and to its District.

In 2006, the 83rd anniversary theme was "How Big Do You Want to Grow?" Bethel strives to build a new church and function as the beacon which warns the ship (our church and community) of any impending dangers, lighting the way for the weary and providing a safe haven.

From *Taking the Old Path and Preserving Our Legacy*, compiled by Florence Hargrave Curtis, Western New York African Methodist Episcopal Conference District 1, Historiographer

Calvary Baptist Church
1184 Genesee Street
Buffalo, New York

Sunday, February 20, 1938 was the official birthday of Mount Calvary Baptist Church. Located at 616 Clinton Street, it was under the leadership of Reverend Collins N. Polite. Approximately four months later, Reverend Polite was called to pastor a church in Philadelphia. On Sunday, September 18, 1938, Reverend Peter Trammell, a native of Lafayette, Alabama, was installed as the new pastor of Mount Calvary Baptist Church. Reverend Trammell was a mild-mannered, gentle speaking, kindhearted man who possessed the innate quality of leadership along with a radar-like instinct that strongly influenced the success of his pastorate. The first Deacon and Trustee Boards along with the  church school were established under the leadership of Reverend Trammell. His vision led to the creation of numerous auxiliaries including B.T.U., Junior Choir, Good Samaritan Club, Usher Boards, Young Adult Choir, Number 1 Choir, Radio Choir, Men's Chorus, Missionary, Mothers and Daughters Club, Nurses, Baptizing Committee, and Education Committee.

The church moved to 476 William Street on April 1, 1939 and moved again to 245 Spring Street on June 22, 1940. On August 29, 1940 the church was incorporated but due to a typographical error the "Mount" was omitted and the church officially became the "Calvary Baptist Church." The first mortgage burning ceremony took place on November 7, 1943. As the church membership continued to increase it became evident that a larger dwelling place was needed. In February 1947, a giant step was taken in the purchasing of a vacant lot at 539 William Street and the groundbreaking ceremony for the new church was held on April 13th of the same year.

The first service was held in the newly completed basement on October 3, 1948. The church was finally completed September 23, 1951, but additions were added in 1952, 1958 (the mortgage was also burned this year), and in 1960.
After 24 years of faithful and dedicated leadership to the Calvary Baptist Church, Reverend Peter Trammell passed away to glory.

Reverend L.T. Boyce of Memphis, Tennessee was selected as the new pastor of the Calvary Baptist Church and was installed on September 22, 1963. Under his administration the church's membership grew tremendously. Reverend Boyce always displayed courage and a steadfast faith in God. These, combined with delightful sense of humor and a background of thorough training in Baptist doctrine, were his sources of strength. Reverend Boyce's leadership enabled Calvary to take an active role in the Great Lakes Association, the Empire State Missionary Convention, and the National Baptist Convention, U.S.A. The purchase of a new piano, sound system, parsonage, the creation of the Long Range Building Fund program, the purchase of the present property at 1184 Genesee Street in 1972, the establishment of the Combined Choirs, Youth Encampment, the Norman Fuller Memorial Scholarship, the purchase of a church van, and the building of two parking lots were all accomplished during Reverend Boyce's pastorate. After nearly 28 years of untiring, dedicated service, on July 13, 1991, God called Reverend L.T. Boyce home, ending another chapter in the life of Calvary Baptist Church.

On October 26, 1992, Reverend Troy A. Bronner was called to pastor Calvary Baptist Church. Under Pastor Bronner's very capable leadership, 16 new ministries were added: Discipleship, Keeping Watch, Visitation, Athletic, Hospitality, Mass Choir, Rites of Passage, Security, Wounded Healers, Women Ministry, Audio-Visual, Education, United Nurses, Philemon, and the United Ushers. The church also continued to support active Girl Scouts and Boy Scouts Troops, Tutorial Program, Adult Education Program, Effective Parenting Classes, and a formal discipleship-training program. An administration capability was advanced with the modernization of office equipment.

In 1998, the Mothers' Board was consecrated under Pastor-Teacher Bronner. An increase in membership during Pastor Bronner's pastorate led to the addition of an early morning worship service. Along with daily morning worship at 6:00 a.m. and evening worship at 6:00 p.m., "Friday Night Alive" was introduced in 1998 to provide an opportunity for ministries in training to share God's word.

Other ministries added to carry out the mission of the church were Marriage Enrichment, Young Women's and Young Married Women's Fellowship, Litany, Dance, Cooking, Evangelistic, and Senior Care. In preparation of the new millennium, Calvary developed a comprehensive Strategic Plan for the church.

In October 1999, Reverend Troy A. Bronner was called to establish the Elim Christian Fellowship, closing another chapter in the life of Calvary Baptist Church.

Reverend David A. Keaton MDiv. of Roanoke, Virginia was elected as the new pastor of Calvary Baptist Church in August 2001.His God-inspired vision for Calvary in the 21st Century was "Going Back to the Old Landmark." Pastor Keaton developed a series of Bible Institutes on Tuesdays using the themes: Jesus, the Bible, Fasting, and Evangelism. www.calvarybaptistchurch.org

In November 2010, Reverend Quinton Chad Foster, MDiv., was selected as the new pastor of Calvary Baptist Church. A native Houstonian and fifth generation preacher/pastor, Reverend Foster acknowledged his call to preach at the age of twelve. His goal is to continue to help the congregation to have an appetite for the Word of God, an ambition for the Will of God, and to be active in the Work of God.

Calvary Christian Methodist Episcopal Church
1007 Ellicott Street
Buffalo, New York

Calvary Christian Methodist Episcopal (C.M.E) Church formerly known as Mount Olive C.M.E. Church was organized in 1920 in a house at 25 Potter Street (now named Nash Street), under the leadership of Reverend M.D. Moon. Reverend R.A. Carter was Bishop and Reverend Denson was Presiding Elder. The charter members were Mr. & Mrs. William (Annabelle) Stokes, Mr. & Mrs. Roosevelt (Ruth) Jarrett, Mr. & Mrs. George (Lucille) Rogers, Mr. & Mrs. Louie (Blanche) Wilson, Mr. Branch, Mrs. Maxwell and Mrs. Addie Morris. In 1944, under Reverend Pilgrim's pastorate, the church was remodeled with the installation of a choir balcony over the pulpit.

Reverend M.L. Littlejohn was assigned to pastor the church in 1946. In 1949, the congregation purchased a church at 117 Pratt Street, with a parsonage in the rear, and renamed the church Jubilee Temple C.M.E. Church. In 1955, Reverend F.E. Bell was appointed pastor and the church membership was split. Most of church's members followed Reverend Littlejohn to form a new church. In 1959, Jubilee Temple was sold to the Buffalo Municipal Housing Authority.

At that time the building at 1007 Ellicott was purchased and named Calvary C.M.E. Church. Through it all the church has stood firm.

The following ministers have pastored the church to date.

1920-1922	Reverend M.D. Moon	1922-1924	Reverend Pendleton
1924-1926	Reverend Grigg	1926-1927	Reverend Thrike
1927-1929	Reverend Harris	1929-1932	Reverend A.P. Porter
1932-1935	Reverend Walker	1935-1939	Reverend Clark
1939-1940	Reverend Fuller	1940-1941	Reverend Linder
1941-1946	Reverend U.L. Pilgrim	1946-1955	Reverend Littlejohn
1955-1961	Reverend F.E. Bell	1961-1964	Reverend A.Crumbley
1964-1966	Reverend H.R. Delaney	1966-1967	Reverend T. McBeth
1967-1975	Reverend J. Lightsey	1975-1983	Reverend J. Hadley
1983-1986	Reverend J.A. Sabb	1986-1988	Reverend J. Taylor
1988-1992	Reverend A. Singh	1992-2000	Reverend M. Bolden
2000-2004	Reverend Edgerton	2004-2007	Reverend N. O'Neal
2007-2010	Reverend R. Reese-Young		
2010	Reverend Dr. W.A. Williams		

The history of Calvary C.M.E. Church would not be complete if we did not pay tribute to these people of God, for they were faithful in their commitment to carry out the gospel of Jesus the Christ. Through His word, we continue to minister to the unsaved. Calvary C.M.E. Church is a church that is striving to be *An Essential Church: Poised For 21st Century Ministry.*

Centennial African Methodist Episcopal Zion Church
127 Doat Street
Buffalo, New York

I n 1974, the Reverend Walter Patton, then a member of St. Luke Zion Church, Buffalo, New York, was inspired by God to organize a new African Methodist Episcopal Zion Church. He expressed the idea to the Right Reverend Herbert Bell Shaw, Presiding Prelate of the First Episcopal

District. Bishop Shaw promised the assistance to the Western New York Conference if Reverend Patton could locate an available church with a committed membership.

In 1975, the property at 125-127 Doat Street was purchased by the WNY Conference with the Conference paying half of the purchase price and the local church assuming the remaining half. At the 1975 Annual Conference, Reverend Patton was appointed the first pastor of this yet unnamed African Methodist Episcopal Zion Church. The first official service was the Missionary Candlelight Service on Friday evening of the Annual Conference.

The name CENTENNIAL came from the collective thoughts of Bishop Shaw and the Reverend Andrew Whitted, Pastor of St. Luke. It was the 125th anniversary of the WNY Conference, the bicentennial year of the United States and reminded

Reverend Whitted of Greater Centennial African Methodist Episcopal Zion Church, Mt. Vernon, New York in the New York Conference. With a new church and thirty-four members, Reverend Patton began his work.

During his pastorate, from 1975-1977, many needed repairs were made to the church building. In 1977, the Reverend Samuel Harris was appointed as pastor until 1979. Centennial was privileged to host the 1979 District Conference during Reverend Harris' pastorate. During the 1979 Annual Conference, the Reverend Maceo M. Freeman was appointed to lead Centennial. On the first Sunday Service of his pastorate, twenty new members were added.

Most of them transferred from Durham Memorial African Methodist Episcopal Zion Church Buffalo, New York. With an active membership of approximately forty adults, Centennial set its sights in new directions that would lead the church to where God would will for Centennial to go. Later in 1979, the magnificent Voices Of Centennial combined to sing praises as Centennial's Gospel Choir.

Daniel Freeman served as the first organist to the choir. Between the years of 1979 and 1980 many physical improvements were made; the sanctuary ceiling was repaired and painted and the dining hall and kitchen were remodeled. This was done by Reverend Freeman and Brothers James Freeman, William Robinson, Willis Mack, Jessie Felton, John Harrell and others.

The women of the church also participated in beautifying the sanctuary. New pulpit vestments were made by Sister Raynette Robinson; candelabras for the altar were purchased by Sister Eula Lucas-Williams; communion rail draperies were made by Sister Linda Harris; and the Trustee Board, led by the chairperson, Sister Winifred Marshall carpeted the entire pulpit area. In 1980, a new organ was purchased and a longstanding debt was paid in full. Also in 1980, the church was honored by the visits of The Right Reverend Reuben L. Speaks who visited in January and the Right Reverend J. Clinton Hoggard made Centennial his first Episcopal visit in July as the newly appointed Presiding Prelate of the conference. The Centennial Children's Choir was founded by Sister Margret Hawkins and Brother James Anthony Freeman.

Evangelism was the theme in 1981 and on several Sundays the members, armed with the Holy Spirit, went to the "hedges and byways" of the church neighborhood to "compel them to come." The efforts were successful in that they let people know that Centennial was alive and thriving! Many of the neighborhood children began attending Sunday School.

During that year Reverend Freeman an accomplished vocalist and musician, was presented in concert. In 1982, Centennial extended its arms to the community by establishing a food pantry to accommodate those in need. The Youth Enrichment Program was established to teach and nurture young people. An exercise class was started to promote healthy living.

By 1983, Centennial's membership had increased to 140 members. Reverend Freeman had continued to be reappointed each year since 1979 and continued to institute exciting and meaningful programs. One of the highlights of the year was a visit from Sister Alcestis Coleman, the General President of the Women's Home and Overseas Missionary Society, as the Women's Day Speaker. A year of spiritual growth, 1983 saw two members presented Local Preacher's Licenses - Brother Willie Overall and Sister Sylvia Hall, and Centennial held its first Sunday School class with Sister Hall as Superintendent. 1984 began as a year of severe national economic crises with many unemployed in the area. Reverend Freeman pursued the idea of starting a lunch kitchen to feed the hungry. He would take part in preparation and cooking to feed those who were in need. He was noted saying "Those who would lead must first serve." The number of people fed increased each week.

The emphasis in the early months of 1984 was to discharge Centennial's share of the mortgage on the church and parsonage. The drive was spearheaded by Sister Edna Pryor, Maymel Harrell and Hassie Robinson. In early May, the final payment was made. On May 29, 1984, during services in which Bishop Hoggard presided, the mortgage was burned. By 1985, the young voices of Centennial continued to grow. Seeing a need to utilize the zeal of the youth Centennial's youth choir was formed from the older voices of Centennial's children's Choir, under the guidance of Sister Joan Harris and the direction of Brother James A. Freeman. By 1987 the Bailey-Doat area was rapidly becoming an area populated with crime. Drugs and prostitution became common to the area. Reverend Freeman began a campaign to save our youth and Centennial's youth began to flourish. Reverend Freeman knew that it was up to the membership of Centennial to save the youth. That year Centennial's Youth Council was formed under the guidance of Brother James A. Freeman.

By 1989, the interior of the sanctuary had begun to deteriorate. Many repairs and improvements were needed. Reverend Freeman who walked by faith and not by sight decided to go forward with the contracting for the much needed repairs. He began the rally for the building fund. He appealed to the congregation who all pitched in as a church family to rebuild the new church home. The congregation worshipped and watched the old slowly turn into the new. Reverend Freeman and the men of Centennial members rolled up their sleeves and helped in order to help defray the cost. With constant prayer and had work, by 1990 Centennial was blessed with a brand new sanctuary.

In 1990, Centennial served as host to the 140th Session of the Western New York Annual Conference. Bishop J. Clinton Hoggard was the Presiding Prelate and Reverend Joseph Davis

Kerr was the Presiding Elder. The sanctuary was filled with ministers and lay persons from all over Western New York. During a 1991 dedication service of the new stained glass panel behind the pulpit, Reverend Freeman decided to dedicate it to Reverend Walter Patton, the founding minister of Centennial. During this service a special offering was collected and The Walter Patton Scholarship Fund was founded. In 1991, the Centennial Children's Choir, under the direction of Brenda Chandler, was renamed the Centennial Joy Bells by Reverend Freeman. In the same year, Brother James Anthony Freeman delivered his powerful and uplifting trial sermon. He received his local preacher's license in 1992.

During 1992, Brother Adolphus Allen and his wife Dorcus (Dolly) became Centennial's Minister of Music and assistant. They blessed Centennial with their ministry through music. The Reverend Maceo McDonald Freeman served the Centennial congregation faithfully for 24 years until the Lord called him home from labor to reward. At the time of Reverend Freeman's untimely death in October 2003, he held the distinction of being Centennial's longest tenured Pastor.

On the second Sunday in October, the Reverend Craig W. Douglass was asked by Presiding Elder, Reverend Robert E. Williams to bring the morning message. Reverend Douglass was an associate minister at the Walls Memorial African Methodist Episcopal Zion Church, Buffalo, New York. Over the years, Reverend Douglass had filled in for Reverend Freeman in his absence.

During that next week in October, Reverend Douglass met with the Presiding Elder and was asked to continue holding down the pulpit until Bishop George W.C. Walker, Sr. could make an official appointment. Reverend Douglass agreed and he and his wife, Yvonne came in with one question on their minds, "What can we do to help?" From 2003, Pastor and Lady Douglass have moved Centennial with care, compassion, and commitment to

God and His people. Together with their four children, Ebony, Amber, David, and Jonathan, they continue to trust in God, knowing that the best is yet to come. http://www.wix.com/centennial/buffalo/

Damascus Baptist Church
210 24th Street
Niagara Falls, New York

D amascus Baptist Church was founded in 1974 under the leadership of Pastor Eugene Phelps. At that time, he was the pastor of Mount Sinai Baptist Church in Niagara Falls, New York. Pastor Phelps felt the need to relocate from Mount Sinai. He and several followers started Damascus Baptist Church. After his death, several pastors led the flock including Pastor Bradley and Pastor Brown.

"When the time came for a new leader, I, Pastor Joseph Jones, was an associate minister at Mount Erie Baptist Church on

Fairfield Avenue in Niagara Falls. I was called to be the pastor at Damascus in March 1985. At that time there were three members. The first Sunday I preached there two were in attendance." The church was using a building that was once a jewelry store and in 1992, Pastor Jones and members launched an expansion program. With much prayer, hard work, and help from members and the community, the present building was completed.

We, at Damascus Baptist Church, are an open and inviting community of believers who seek to help one another to follow Christ with deeper commitment. We encourage one another to respond to the call of the Holy Spirit, to live the gospel by living lives in imitation of our Lord, Jesus Christ.

We strive to live, teach, and share the idea that our church as a family and a very real sense. Just as members of the traditional family look out for one another and share one another's joy and sorrow, we likewise are concerned with spiritual growth, development, and well-being of all our sisters and brothers who make up our church community. Through the intercession of Jesus Christ, the holy spirit of our church, we dedicate all our words and actions to the glory of God our father.

At Damascus Baptist Church, we strive to minister not only to our members but also to the surrounding community. In addition to our regular services, we have a youth program that emphasizes education and excellence. Our annual education awards banquet honors our students for accomplishments in school. We also sponsor field trips for our youth to interesting places for fun and for learning. We have revivals each year with dynamic guest speakers, inspiring music and uplifting fellowship. We recently began our Every Little Bit Helps mission whereby people in the community who are in need may receive assistance. Our church family enjoys many dinners and special programs throughout the year where we celebrate holiday special occasions and important events.

We are currently undertaking another expansion project. Plans were drawn up for new sanctuary, the parking area, revamped classroom space and an updated Fellowship Hall. We need the continued support not only from our church members but from the entire community, so that with God's help and blessing, we will see our vision for new and better church come to fruition.

Our church school is at 9:30 a.m. on Sunday followed by worship service at 11:00 a.m. Bible and prayer service is held on Wednesday at 7 p.m. Youth service is held every fourth Sunday and Community Prayer service at noon every Friday. We invite all to come and worship and grow with us.

Delaine Waring African Methodist
Episcopal Church
680 Swan Street
Buffalo, New York

In June 1952, the Annual Conference convened at Bethel African Methodist Episcopal Church, Buffalo, New York. The Presiding Bishop George W. Barber gave the Reverend Joseph A. Delaine of Clarendon, South Carolina an open appointment and a commission to organize a second church in Buffalo. It was named in memory of Judge J. Waites Waring and Pastor Joseph Delaine. On July 2, 1956, Delaine Waring African Methodist Episcopal Church was organized and at the first service held in the Meadows Funeral Home, twenty eight persons joined. Reverend Otis Outen succeeded Reverend Delaine in 1957.

The congregation worshiped at Liberty Baptist Church and later at the Christian Center at 280 Hickory Street until April 1961. With the assistance of Presiding Elder J. W. Moses and the New York Annual Conference, the congregation was successful in purchasing the building at 680 Swan Street. In December 1961, the Reverend O. Urcile Ifil, Sr. was appointed to continue its growth. During his tenure, Delaine Waring was renamed St. Matthew African Methodist Episcopal Church.

In November 1964, at the Fall Convocation hosted by Bethel African Methodist Episcopal Church, New York City, Reverend S. Frank Emmanuel was appointed pastor. Under his administration, a resolution to return the church's name to Delaine Waring was introduced. In May 1965, Bishop Bright honored this resolution at the New York Annual Conference. In April 1966, the name was officially changed to the bane of the original Delaine Waring African Methodist Episcopal Church.

Following Reverend Emmanuel in 1968 was Reverend Floyd Black in 1969; Reverend Theodore Hudson, 1969-1970; Reverend C.M. Huff, 1970-1971; Reverend G. Grant Crumply (Supervising Pastor Bethel African Methodist Episcopal) 1971-1972; Reverend John Caper, 1974-1977; Reverend Henry Lewis, 1977-1984; Reverend Henry Wynn, 1984-1991; Reverend William Simon 1991; Reverend John Rolls, 1991-1992.

The Reverend Robert L. Reynolds served as pastor for fifteen years after being appointed by Bishop Frank Cummings in 1992 at the New York Annual Conference. He raised the spiritual level of the membership and orchestrated the renovation of the fellowship hall and the parsonage. Additionally, in 1996, Reverend Reynolds and Delaine Waring hosted the first Episcopal Organizational meeting which established the Western New York Conference.
It also hosted the Sixth Session of the Western New York Annual Conference in 2003 as well as the Western New York District Conference in 2006. Pastor Reynolds served as Statistical Secretary for the Western New York Annual Conference and as an instructor at the Western New York Ministerial Institute.

Early in 2007, Reverend A. Iona Smith Nze was appointed as pastor   and director of public relations at the Eleventh Western New York Annual Conference at Baber African Methodist Episcopal Church in Rochester, NY.

Reverend Nze is the first woman pastor of Delaine Waring in the history of the church.

From *Taking the Old Path and Preserving Our Legacy*, compiled by Florence Hargrave Curtis, Western New York African Methodist Episcopal Conference District 1, Historiographer

Deliverance Temple Church of God in Christ
177 Sherman Street
Buffalo, New York

In 1963, after twenty years of faithful service and worship at Holy Temple Church of God in Christ, under the pastorate of the late Bishop E.F. McClellan, Elder Lincoln Williams, Sr. was led by the Lord to start a church. Moving under the junction of the Holy Spirit on September 15, 1963, Elder Williams officially opened the doors of Deliverance Temple Church of God In Christ to all mankind, beginning with only his wife and nine children.

The Lord honored the faith of Elder Williams and added to the church so much that it was necessary to move to a larger edifice. In 1965, Deliverance Temple moved to 643 William Street. In 1968, Deliverance Temple was blessed to obtain a facility at 704 William Street. This location served as a testimony to this body of believers' desire to serve the Lord in excellence, unity of spirit and purpose as the membership quickly united to complete extensive renovations to the facility. The Word of the Lord was preached with power and authority: many souls were saved, delivered, healed and filled with the gift of the Holy Ghost "…and the Lord added to the church daily, those who were being saved."

In 1983, the Lord again honored Elder Williams and the Deliverance Temple Church family by blessing them to purchase the palatial edifice at 177 Sherman Street, the current home of Deliverance Temple Church of God in Christ. Upon entering the Sherman Street edifice, the Pastor and congregation implemented a renovation plan which included the Pastor's study, several new offices, electrical services, plumbing, facilities for men and women, carpeting, complete restructuring of the pulpit and choir areas, exterior paving of a parking area for the congregation and restoration of the beautiful mosaic glass windows. Under Elder Williams' leadership, the church increased its holdings to include the properties at 175 and 179 Sherman Street and 212 Peckham Street.

It is a faithful saying that "the Lord has done great things for us; wherein we are glad." Psalm 126:3. Deliverance Temple is grateful to God for his blessing as continuity of leadership played a major role its success. The Lord blessed Elder Williams, Sr. to lead   for almost one half century. His work and leadership will never be forgotten. In August 2007, Bishop Frank White appointed Elder Gregory Webster as Pastor. His appointment was confirmed and he was installed as the church's Senior Pastor on Saturday, September 26, 2009.

> *How firm a foundation, ye saints of the Lord,*
> *is laid for your faith in his excellent word!*
> *What more can he say than to you he hath said,*
> *to you that for refuge to Jesus have fled?*
>
> *"Fear not, I am with thee; O be not dismayed!*
> *For I am thy God, and will still give thee aid;*
> *I'll strengthen thee, help thee,*
> *and cause thee to stand.*

The whole of Jesus' own preaching, teaching, and ministry centered in the words, "The Kingdom of God is at hand." Mark 1:15. The kingdom of God is connected to Deliverance Temple's past, present and future by an all powerful God who is able to make all grace abound. As Deliverance Temple moves through the 21st Century and prepares for a latter day ministry, the church leadership continues to build upon the firm foundation established der the leadership and founder, Elder Lincoln Williams.

Deliverance Temple Church of God in Christ engages to authoritatively and courageously represent the Lord Jesus Christ and the kingdom of God through the preached Word, anointed worship, dynamic witness and spirit led works. We further engage to empower individuals, couples and families to discover and make evident the power of the Holy Spirit in day-to-day living. We will stand and bless the Lord our God forever and ever!

Submitted by Deliverance Temple Church of God in Christ

Durham Memorial African Methodist Episcopal Zion Church
174 East Eagle Street
Buffalo, New York

The building that houses Durham Memorial Church was built in 1922-23 as the new home of St. Luke's African Methodist Episcopal Zion Church. Our congregation, a splinter group of St. Luke's, was formed in 1958 specifically to remain in this building after St. Luke's, by then a much larger congregation, had voted to move to more spacious quarters elsewhere in the city. The historical roots of Durham Memorial African Methodist Episcopal Zion Church go back to 1831 when the Colored Methodist Society, Buffalo's first black religious organization, was established. All African-American congregations in Buffalo descend from either this society or from a separate Baptist congregation that dates from about the same time.

From the Colored Methodist Society evolved many other religious organizations including People's Reformed Methodist Church. That congregation reorganized in 1906 and joined the African Methodist Episcopal Zion Church under the name St. Luke's African Methodist Episcopal Zion Church. It remodeled a building on Michigan Avenue into one of the finest structures owned by blacks in Buffalo. The growing congregation and its related activities placed a tremendous strain on the church. After the Reverend Henry Durham was appointed as the new pastor in 1914, the congregation embarked on building a new complex that would provide both a larger and more dignified sanctuary, as well as an education building for the congregation's extensive programs. The church purchased a lot on East Eagle Street, just east of downtown, and construction began in 1922 with the cornerstone being laid on Palm Sunday. The first service in the new church was held a year later on Easter Sunday.

This new edifice, built at a cost of $57,000, was the first church building in Buffalo to be built by a black congregation and was, for years, the largest African-American church building in the city. Because of the building's size, numerous black congregations would hold their annual state meetings here, and Masonic groups would use it for their large public services.

Designed by Louis Greenstein, it is a brick and cast-stone Neo-Gothic structure with a squat bell tower to the side. Although the congregation completed the church, it did not raise enough money to construct the educational wing. This severely curtailed the congregation's ability to continue its various social programs. While Pastor Durham and the members hoped that money would become available later, 1957 still had not raised the funds for the educational wing, and the congregation had outgrown its church.

With membership approaching 1,000, the congregation considered plans for building an addition, remodeling the existing facility, or relocating. After weighing these options, the congregation voted to relocate and purchased a building elsewhere in Buffalo. However, some members did not agree with this decision. This group petitioned Bishop William J. Walls to organize a new African Methodist Episcopal Zion Society that could remain at the East Eagle Street site, and the request was granted. Out of respect for the man who had served as pastor when the church was being built, the congregation named the new society the Henry Durham

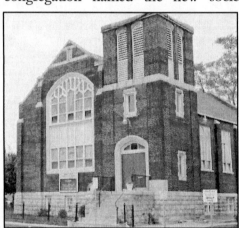

Memorial African Methodist Episcopal Zion Church. The building was sold to the reorganized con-gregation for $20,000 and on Palm Sunday, March 31, 1958, the first worship service was held with Presiding Elder Arthur E. May delivering the sermon.

The new congregation chose to keep alive, Pastor Durham's dream of ministering to the people of this section of Buffalo. An important, even essential part of this dream was to provide space needed to house the programs and services that are such an important part of black congregations.

Over the years, R.W. Christian (1905-1906), John C. Taylor 1906-1914, Henry Durham 1914-1926; B.C. VanBuren1926-1929; E. Rex Flack 1929-1932; Stephen Spottswood 1932-1946; Derrick M. Byrd,Sr. 1936-1938; Nicholas D. King 1938-1943; E. Franklin Jackson 1943-1952; Hunter B. Bess 1952-1958.

Pastors have come and gone each wanting to complete the dreams of those before them. In the late 1960s and early 1970s, the congregation raised money, which it set aside for a new educational building/community center that would also have included a senior citizens center. Groundbreaking ceremonies were held, but no further progress was made. Henry Durham's vision continued to be a dream. During these years the neighborhood changed as well. When the church was built, the neighborhood consisted of single- and two-family homes; however, urban renewal brought dramatic changes in the 1950s and 1960s.

Most of the houses were torn down and replaced by tall apartment buildings, or "projects," which destroyed the old sense of community in the neighborhood.

Throughout this upheaval, the church remained a beacon, providing a constant source of hope and assistance, and serving the needs of both new and old residents. Reverend Richard Stewart became pastor of the congregation in June 1990. A "son" of Durham Memorial, he had been a member of St. Luke's congregation when he was growing up. His family lived on Union Street (which no longer exists) one block from the church; the new hospital occupies that location today.

Being a native son, he appreciated the building, its status in Buffalo's African-American history, and the church's early mandate to minister to the community. He, too, tried to be a catalyst in fulfilling the dreams of his predecessors; they envisioned this church as a spiritual haven, a place for educational and community service, and a center for the black community. He strongly believed that the types of ministry and programs that Pastor Durham sought to offer in the early 1900s were needed then more than ever.

The congregation's community presence and outreach increased in response to neighborhood changes. We have expanded our programming, by opening a soup kitchen in 1990 and over 175,000 meals have been served to date.

We provide Legal Aid assistance on a weekly basis; the Veterans Association Homeless task force visits monthly; we provide meeting space for Alcoholics Anonymous; we mount voter registration drives every year; and we offer AIDS education and counseling. Scouting programs help keep young people off the streets and foster a sense of discipline and responsibility. Now with over 200 members, our congregation is stable; it is even growing, and we find ourselves to be the nucleus around which a new community is being developed. The vision of those who stayed when St. Luke's moved is being proved many times over.

Because he embraced Reverend Durham's vision, Reverend Stewart embarked on a campaign to "Complete the Dream" soon after his appointment as pastor. As with any worthwhile endeavor, he believed that we must go back to the roots that we had to be firmly grounded. He began a search for church records and information about the church's history from its beginnings in 1831.

His goal was twofold: to create a written record of this congregation and its building, and to educate the current membership about the important roles our congregation and this building have played in the history of Buffalo and the city's African-American community.

Durham is going forward with our roots firmly grounded in our heritage - not just our heritage as the oldest church building constructed for African Americans in Buffalo - but also our tradition as a spiritual and social center serving the city's African-American community. www.sacredplaces.org

The Durham Memorial A.M.E. Zion Church's Community Outreach Center is host to many activities and services that benefit the health of the Buffalo community, including the Central City Café. It has been in weekly operation since 1990 and is one of the largest soup kitchens in the city. The Outreach Center opened in 2003, and it has a kitchen and dining area for 150 people and a gym and multi-purpose room seating up to 400, and a day-care center.

Reverend Stewart retired in 2009 and he went from labor to reward in February 2010.

Reverend George C. Woodruff currently serves as the pastor of Durham.

Elim Christian Fellowship
70 Chalmers Avenue
Buffalo, New York

If you return to me and obey my commands, then, even if your exiled people are of the farthest horizons; I will gather them from there and bring them to the place I have chosen as a dwelling for my name. (Nehemiah 1:9-NIV)And they came to ELIM, where there were twelve wells of water and seventy palm trees and they encamped there by the waters (Exodus 15:27)

ELIM Christian Fellowship was established on November 7, 1999, under the inspiration of God to the visionary and Senior Pastor T. Anthony Bronner. Elim Christian Fellowship, Inc. is a non-denominational, multi-cultural, bible-based ministry engaged in Spirit-filled worship that touches the heart of God, preaches and teaches with integrity the word of God, and equips the saints to do the work of Jesus Christ to evangelize the world.

The name ELIM conceptually means a place of refreshing, reviving, and renewing for weary travelers. ELIM has proven to be a fitting symbol of spiritual revitalization and restoration.

On the first day of worship at the Buffalo Christian Center over seven hundred people committed their head, heart and hand to God's vision for Elim Christian Fellowship. Many of those who joined were regular attendees of the Regional Morning Prayer, which assembled every morning from 5:30 a.m. to 8:30 a.m. ELIM Christian Fellowship was birthed out of

this Regional Morning Prayer Movement which has continued uninterrupted for the past ten years. ELIM soon outgrew the facilities at the Buffalo Christian Center and relocated to Turner Carroll High School on February 7, 2000. After only six months in existence, Elim's membership doubled. The current active membership is in excess of sixteen hundred members and progressively growing.

Recent numbers indicate that on average approximately fifty persons per month choose to make ELIM Christian Fellowship their spiritual home. Thus, this steady stream of new members would suggest that ELIM has great potential for new growth and longevity. In June 2000, Elim Christian Fellowship purchased property for the construction of the new Worship and Youth Center. The Groundbreaking Ceremony took place on August 26, 2000 with over seven hundred grateful members, community and political well-wishers present.

Members and visitors of ELIM had the opportunity to pray for wisdom and guidance on October 29, 2000, for First Lady of the United States, Hillary R. Clinton as she continued to pursue public service. We were inspired by her visit and her words of encouragement. To further fulfill God's Great Commission, ELIM Christian Fellowship of Rochester, New York also under the leadership of Senior Pastor T. Anthony Bronner, was birthed on Sunday, November 17, 2002. The expansion of Elim Christian Fellowship into the Rochester community was an "evolution not a revolution." It was a natural progression for a dynamic, forward-thinking ministry that is only bound by its leadership's desire to win souls for Christ. The next few years produced an outpour and influx of what was coined as "permanent visitors" from other churches from all denominations due to the unconventional time of worship service beginning at 2:00 pm.

The congregation continued to expand over the next two years which led to the expansion relocation and purchase of our current worship center. On September 13, 2004, ELIM

Rochester officially acquired property on the east side of Rochester.

On Sunday, April 30, 2006, ELIM Buffalo opened the doors of the new Worship Center with a service of thanksgiving. On this day the leaders and congregational members of ELIM gathered in the Central Park Plaza were they prayed and released a thousand balloons into the community with the message that "God in Not an option." After the release the crowd of approximately one thousand marched over to the new edifice. By the grace of the Almighty God, on October 11, 2008, ELIM Christian Fellowship & Turning the World Upside Down Covenant Fellowship, Inc. proudly witnessed the Consecration and Ordination Service for Bishop T. Anthony Bronner by The Right Reverend David Michael Copeland.

He serves as Presiding Prelate of the Kingdom Council of Interdependent Christian Churches and Ministries, Inc. of San Antonio, Texas. Numerous dignitaries, family and friends from all across the county attended, excited that God in His infinite wisdom, called Pastor Bronner of Buffalo, New York to the Bishopric. ELIM is known for its spirit-led praise & worship, and intercessory prayer. People from all races, religions, age groups and denominational affiliations gather weekly to seek God's face. A highlight of ELIM is its thriving youth ministry. ELIM's dedicated staff of youth pastors provides life-changing instruction for the youth of our neighboring communities.

ELIM Christian Fellowship is an instrument by which God uses His vessel, Bishop T. Anthony Bronner, to bring to the communities of Buffalo and Rochester, the region of Western New York, and eventually the world, refreshing worship, passionate prayer, and the word of God preached with integrity.

"Oh God, remember ELIM with favor and allow your name to dwell there." Nehemiah 1:8B, 13:31.

Submitted by Elim Christian Fellowship

Enter In Ministries Full Gospel Baptist Church
1761 Genesee Street
Buffalo, New York

Enter In Ministries Full Gospel Baptist Church was conceived on May 3, 2009 and we began to worship at the True Bethel Baptist Church Campus at 907 E. Ferry Street until we located our own place of worship. Our name "Enter In" was derived from Psalms 100:4. Our church theme is "With love and kindness have I drawn thee."

Pastor Rosetta Swain serves as the first Pastor of the Enter In Ministries Full Gospel Baptist Church, and she successfully completed the Greater Refuge Temple Bible College Institute Academy with a biblical degree and Houghton College Pastoral Studies and Counseling.

We officially became Enter In Ministries Full Gospel Baptist Church in November 2009 with a certificate by our Presiding Bishop, Paul S. Morton; our Regional Bishop, Kenneth Robinson and our State Overseer, Darius G. Pridgen of Full Gospel Baptist Church Fellowship International.

On December 20, 2009, we were blessed to find our present

location at 1761 Genesee Street at the corner of Rawlins in Buffalo, NY. We are presently at this location with our officers and founding members: Elder Danielle Easley, Church Program Coordinator; Elder Clifford Jackson, Assisting Elder; Donald Madding, Financial Treasurer; James Woodruff, Trustee; Bernadette Hicks, Deaconess; LaVita J. Spentz,

Secretary; Shelly Jackson, Church Clerk; Cheryl Jackson, Hospitality; Jennifer Inniss, Children's Ministry. On September 26, 2010 we were honored to elevate in ordination our first Minister Clifford Jackson to Elder.

Our Sunday services start with Sunday School at 11:00 am, worship service at 12 noon, and the Back to Basics Bible Study on Tuesdays at 7:00 pm. Pastor Swain has hosted a weekly television show on Public Access for the past 25 years, "Sounding the Trumpet." The program is now aired on Sunday afternoons at 3:30pm.

Photo and history submitted by LaVita Spence

Ephesus Ministries
341 Grider Street
Buffalo, New York

Ephesus Ministries was led in its first worship service on Sunday, March 24, 2002, by its Founders, Pastors Jeff and Deborah Carter. Due to the graciousness of Father Francis (Butch) Mazur, Pastor of the former St. Gerard Parish on Bailey and East Delavan, Ephesus was able to hold Sunday worship services at St. Gerard for the first two years of its humble existence.

For the first year, weekly Bible studies and Prayer services were held in the homes of members of the church. This was an exciting time for Ephesus. Moving from home-to-home caused Ephesus to become a tight-knit family type congregation upon which was built a strong foundation for ministry that would fit the vision of the founder. Sharing this close fellowship allowed the Pastor to lead the congregation into fasting and praying and into a high quality bible study that caused Ephesus to really mature into the vision for which it was named.

Ephesus Ministries was named by Pastor Jeff Carter after the New Testament Church in Ephesus. In the book of Acts, Chapter 19, the Apostle Paul makes a missionary stop in Ephesus. After he leads disciples there into receiving the Holy Ghost, a church so devoted to evangelism develops that in two  years' time, all of Asia Minor is evangelized. Ephesus Ministries is building on that concept. For this church, sharing the love of Christ in every setting is primary. Pastor Carter began the church as he was retiring from serving for 25 years as the

Coordinating Chaplain at the Attica Correctional Facility. After working in institutional ministry for over 25 years, including Chaplaincy at the Erie County Medical Center, Reverend Carter wanted to lead a church into a new and different kind of Ministry. One that was willing to do most of its ministry outside of the walls of the church building.

Ephesus has been very successful in prison ministry, nursing home ministry, hospital ministry, youth ministry, and in ministry in other settings apart from the regular worship and bible study. In 2004, Ephesus Ministries moved into its present home at 341 Grider Street and 80 Durham Avenue. This property, the past home of the St. Bartholomew Parish is a beautiful church with finely crafted wood work that was done by hand when the church was built in the late 1920's. It is one of the premier architectural gems that Buffalo is noted for. The stones that make up the exterior wall are stones that were used as Buffalo was changing its old cobblestone streets to newly paved streets.

Located next door to the Bissonette House and directly across from the Erie County Medical Center, Ephesus Ministries is in a prime location to do the superb ministry of evangelism that it is maturing to uniquely do. With vibrant worship services, high quality bible study, and excellent youth ministry, Ephesus certainly shows itself to be one of the strongest young churches in the city of Buffalo.

Photo and history submitted by Ephesus Ministries

Evangelistic Temple and Community Church Center
92 Hedley Place
Buffalo, New York

The Evangelistic Temple and Community Church Center, Inc. was organized on April 22, 1922, by the late Pastor Lewis W. Holley in his home at 114 Pine Street. At this first meeting, Pastor Holley was elected President; Mrs. M. Thompson, Vice President; Mrs. Lula Long, Secretary; Mrs. P.C.

Colley, Treasurer and Gospel singer; and Mrs. Lillian Black was the pianist. Also present were Mrs. Hannah Holley, Mrs. Rosa Jackson, Mrs. Ida Bagby and Miss Rachel Rice. Reverend Holley was an ordained minister and a member of the Michigan Avenue Baptist Church. He was an Evangelist and believed profoundly in the oneness of God's people. His belief that we Christians could work together, regardless of denomination, led Reverend Holley and his workers to become an independent, non-denomination Church with its own membership.

In 1927, a place for worship was rented at the corner of Pine and Clinton Streets. Reverend Stand, who held his services on Saturdays, allowed Reverend Holley and his congregation use of the church on Sundays. The workers called themselves the Holley Evangelistic Company. As they prospered, The Reverend James Lyons was appointed assistant minister and Mr. James Phillips and Mr. Milton Davis were the Deacons. Mrs. C. A. Sims, Mr. James Phillips and Mrs. M. Thompson were Trustees.

To assist those who wanted to attend Sunday School, Reverend Holley used a cab to pick up children every Sunday. Jimmy and Irvin Green were two of his first Sunday School pupils. Mrs. Hannah Holley and Mrs. Mentie Thompson went about gathering children for religious instructions and like Dorcas of old, they made clothes and bought shoes for those unprepared to attend

At that time, Mrs. Virginia Jones, Mrs. Edna Roberts, Mrs. William Griffin and Mrs. Virginia Bonds joined the workers and helped to build up a thriving Sunday School and Church. Mrs. Edna Roberts became the pianist and Reverend James Cant became associated with Reverend Holley and his work.

The property at 451 Jefferson Avenue was purchased in 1929 and remodeled for a church. The congregation moved into that new location in April 1930, fulfilling the workers' dream, after many years of toil. After moving into the new church on Jefferson, many of the then present members continued to work faithfully and their efforts were supported with new noteworthy members: Mrs. Henrietta Thomas and family, Mrs. Susie Lacey and family, Mary Alyce and Francis Daniels, Mrs. Ossie Bass and family, Bernie Randall, Leila and her brother Lester Robinson, Marian Richards, William Dixon, Mr. Wesley and Mrs. Janie Dixon, Mrs. Chris Rice, Mr. Ralph Durant, and many others.

The church joined the Community Church Council in 1935. It was incorporated in June 1936 and exempted from taxation. At this time, the name Holley was dropped from the church's name. Reverend Holley went to the National Council, which was held in California in 1937.

The Center was purchased in 1943 for recreation and other church uses; this was the last key acquisition made under Reverend Holley's tenure. After a short illness, Reverend Holley passed away June 12, 1944. During Reverend Holley's failing health, Reverend Luscious Bonds, who had also been working with the church prior to Reverend Holley's illness assumed the pastoral duties. In January 1945, Reverend Bonds was elected Pastor. The mortgage on both buildings was paid off in October 1948 and the church gave a mortgage-burning banquet in January 1949. The membership grew, worked and prospered at 451 Jefferson; and then in June 1959, The Evangelistic Temple moved to 92 Hedley Place. Reverend Bonds retired after eighteen years: of service in 1962. It was under his leadership that our present building was purchased. Reverend Warren Doyle Staton served as interim pastor through 1965. Following his term, Reverend L. Johnson became pastor. Under his leadership, he continued the Scholarship Fund, which donates money each year to high school graduates entering college. He also encouraged membership of the Youth and Children's Choir. During his tenure, he resided at the present parsonage located at 52 Blaine Avenue. Reverend Johnson served as pastor until 1971.

In 1972, The Reverend Tommy L. Pressley Jr., a young man and member of the congregation became our minister. He served until December of 1983. He instituted the Friday night youth activities, a basketball team that was part of the Salvation Army League, and we became more active in Foreign Mission activities. Under his leadership, we also became a participant of the UCM Summer Missionary Program. The Reverend James R. Josey was elected minister in July 1984. During his Pastorate, the Gospel Choir was formed.

After serving as interim pastor for several months, our current Pastor, The Reverend George William DuBois was installed on December 7, 1986. He works diligently to raise his congregation's spiritual awareness and also that of culture and heritage. Under Pastor DuBois' leadership and ministerial guidance, three preachers have been licensed, eight deacons and two deaconesses have been ordained and at least thirteen ministries have been established and continue to prosper. With Pastor DuBois' blessings and assistance, in 1992, we honored our founder posthumously and dedicated and named our fellowship hall after the late Pastor Lewis W. Holley.

Evangelistic Temple has grown significantly in the Word, membership and structural maintenance, under Pastor DuBois' twenty-four-and-half years of Godly leadership. To this end we continue, Developing Our Faith in God. Hebrews 11:1, 6.

Submitted by Evangelistic Temple

Faith Baptist Church
626 Humboldt Parkway
Buffalo, New York

The history of the Faith Baptist Church fellowship reads like a page from the book of Acts of the Apostles. It began in an atmosphere of prayer motivated by God and given through a desire on the part of some people who wanted a church in the Cold Springs area of Buffalo. A Christian church that consists of the elements prescribed by the Holy Word of God, the Bible, and recognizes the human qualities found in a fellowship of mankind. Then we can sing with the hymnologist of old:

"Through many dangers, toils and snares, we have already come.
It was grace that brought us safe thus far, and grace wilt lead us home."

At the call of the late Deacon DeWitt Smallwood in January 1955, eleven persons met at the home of Mrs. Artelia Snyder, 123 Waverly Street, to consider the possibility of organizing a missionary Baptist church in the Cold Spring community to provide for their spiritual needs.

They were DeWitt and Georgiana Smallwood, James Voss, Pearl Moore, Kenneth and Mildred Byers, Verna Morton, Lillie Lunsford, Pearl Westbrook, John and Elizabeth Tyson, and Artelia Snyder. Reverend Roscoe M. Mitchell of Tarrytown, New York met with the group to explore the possibilities. The name Faith was suggested by Mrs. Mary Long. The name Faith Baptist was unanimously approved and adopted. Reverend Mitchell was asked to shepherd us, thus becoming Faith's first pastor. Reverend Mitchell asked that we meet on Wednesday, January 17, 1955, at the home of Mr. and Mrs. Paul Morton, 11 Harlow Place to organize said group into a church. The prayer band included DeWitt, Georgiana, and DeWitt Smallwood Jr.,

Patricia and James Smallwood, Mary Christopher, James Voss, Mrs. Ethel Martin, Verna Morton, Mrs. Naylor, Master Derek Morton, Pearl Moore, Pearl Westbrook, John and Elizabeth Tyson, Sadie Hayes, Mrs. Mary Long and Miss Marshall.

The first public worship service was held on February 6, 1955 at 292-94 Glenwood Avenue in Boreal Hall. Pastor Mitchell's first sermon was entitled, "If God be for us, who can be against us?" There were approximately 183 persons present. The offering received was $183.00. The church was incorporated on February 14, 1955 in the presence of Reverend Roscoe Mitchell, Silas Ford, and Pearl Moore.

The church was formally recorded with City of Buffalo on April14, 1955. On May 22, 1955, Faith Baptist Church was formally recognized as an independent Missionary Baptist Church. The Reverend Porter Phillips of Michigan Avenue Baptist Church preached the Recognition Sermon and the chargers were made to the church. The Lord's Supper was served by Reverend Elijah J. Echols,Sr., pastor of the First Shiloh Baptist Church.In August 1955, 142 Hamlin Road was purchased as our parsonage for the Pastor and his family at the cost of $11,000.

Our present site and the house next to the church were purchased in November 1955 for $68,000.00. This house became the next parsonage. Under the leadership of Pastor Mitchell in 1968, the adjacent building was purchased for demolition, in order to provide a building for a day nursery for children. The new wing was dedicated to Dr. Martin Luther King Jr. who visited the church in 1960, at the invitation of Pastor Mitchell. This addition is the Martin Luther King Jr. Memorial Building also houses the Roscoe M. Mitchell Fellowship Hall located on the third floor. Pastor Mitchell led the congregation until ill health forced him to resign in March 1972. The Reverend Johnny Ray Youngblood served as interim pastor from June until December 1972. A dynamic young preacher he moved onto greater heights as a pastor, preacher, teacher and administrator.

In February 1973, the church elected our next pastor, the Reverend Junius W. Cofield Sr., a quiet, serene, and humble man of God. Under his leadership, two ministers were ordained, Reverends Robert L. Bishop and Junius Willard Cofield Jr. Under the leadership of Pastor Cofield, by the grace of God we continued to progress and serve the Lord. The Mitchell-Cofield Scholarship Fund was established, our present communion table and altar furniture were dedicated, and the parking lot was expanded. Our present Noon Day Bible Class is named in Pastor Cofield's honor. He retired in February 1980, leaving the church without a shepherd.

In 1981, the church elected Pastor James R. Banks II. Under his leadership, the church has continued to grow numerically, financially and most importantly, spiritually. Under his leadership, many renovations have been made: painting of the church, remodeling of the bathrooms, purchase of new kitchen equipment and new office equipment, and the installation of glass block windows in the lower auditorium. Three Bible classes were taught, and two ministers were ordained as Elders, Benjamin F. McCullough and Gregory P. Witherspoon. By God's grace, we have also been able to burn our mortgage.

Our shared past has united us in faith and love, and with God's help we will continue to grow in strength and grace. He has made us a beacon of light of faith for such a time as this.

To God be the Glory for the great things He has done.

Submitted by Faith Baptist Church

First African Methodist Episcopal Church
123 South Street
Lockport, New York

In 1835, a meeting was held for the purpose of providing a school for Negro children. It was resolved that $150 be raised to erect a building suitable for a school house and a public place of worship. The church was organized in 1840 and named Zion Methodist Episcopal Church of Lockport on Lot 18 on South Street. Early in its history, the church served its members and the community well in spite of its meager finances.

One of the earliest and most important citizens of Lockport was Mr. Lyman A. Spalding who owned a great deal of land in Lockport and lived on the corner of Spalding and Locust Streets. The house was moved away years ago. On August 21, 1844, Lyman A. Spalding and his wife Amy P. Spalding passed a deed to the "First Society of the African Methodist Episcopal Church." The deed for the land on which the church building on South Street stands was recorded on September 2, 1844 at 4 o'clock. The deed, in safe keeping, names three men described as Trustees: James Morgan, William Sanders, and Woodford Mills.

First African Methodist Episcopal Church has a documented history spanning over 175 years. This is 32 years from the date of the land gift. It is well known that the church served the colored (sic) community well and provided a social and religious center for the early Christians.

History records that the women of First African Methodist Episcopal Baptist Church whose devotion knew no bounds, had little money, but possessed the spirit of determination to keep the church always open. The spirit in these women was undaunted and they took care of their families, worked other jobs, but at night they could be found cleaning the church, baking and cooking to get money to repair the church.

On some Sunday mornings, the congregation had to raise umbrellas to keep from getting wet. The president of the two year old City Missionary Federation, Mrs. George Sewnzy, heard of the plight of First A.M.E. Under her leadership, the women of the church tried to raise the money needed to repair the building. With the aid of the minister and churchgoers, a sufficiently large sum of money was soon raised to completely renovate the church edifice. In its early years, First African Methodist Episcopal Church often struggled, its finances were minimal, but in spite of the struggles, in spite of the leaking roof, in spite of loose windows and outdated doors, in spite of torrential rains and flooding in the basement and because of a will to survive unimpaired by obstacles, the doors of First African Methodist Episcopal Church never closed and the church prospered. Some of the pastors who served First African Methodist Episcopal Church since 1835 and left the mark of their spiritual leadership on the church and community are listed here.

1857	Reverend Henry C. Thomson
1868--1869	Reverend JH Turpin
1871	Reverend Charles W. Mossell
1871	Reverends CC Green, Clark, Chapelle, Baker
1874--1875	Reverend H. Phenix
1876	Reverend Benjamin Franklin
1878--1879	Reverend MP Cole

1880	Reverend WF Townsend
1919	Reverend Joseph D. Ray
1953	Reverend Dr. S. B. Chappell
1957	Reverend Lascelle M. Watts
1959	Reverend James L. Beach
1961	Reverend Dr. Henry I. Lewis
1981	Reverend Samuel J. King
1982	Reverend Pedro Castro
1990	Reverend Gerald H. Hesson

In 2005, Reverend Dolores Wynn was appointed the Pastor of First A.M.E. Church.

From *Taking the Old Path and Preserving Our Legacy*, compiled by Florence Hargrave Curtis, Historiographer, Western New York African Methodist Episcopal Conference District 1

First Baptist Church
320 Ingham Street
Lackawanna, New York

First Baptist Church has an extensive history of standing as a sentry in guiding men, women and children toward our Heavenly Father. It began with the late Reverend A.J. Phillips who organized the First Baptist Church in the year of 1923. With the help of a strong congregation, Reverend Phillips established the Union Baptist Church. Reverend Timothy Boddie followed Reverend Phillips and under his leadership many members were added to the House of the Lord. Reverend Phillip and Reverend Boodie were significantly responsible for the ground breaking organization and the introduction of the First Baptist Church to Lackawanna, New York. Reverend O.C. Thomas followed Reverend Boddie and Reverend D.O. Danley also served as a Shepherd of the Union Baptist Church. Reverend Herny Snead and Reverend F.B. Williamson were both instrumental in assisting the church to progress and grow

stronger in the Lord. The name Union Baptist Church was changed under the tenure of Dr. O.S.P. Thompson and again renamed First Baptist Church. The First Baptist Church is the Mother Church of all Baptist Churches in the city of Lackawanna, New York. Reverend Thompson, a scholar, teacher and preacher foresaw the need to expand the building. Through his administration a beautiful corridor, office and a tall tower were erected with a cross at its pinnacle.

The Reverend William Warfield, an energetic and dynamic preacher succeeded Reverend Thompson. The church continued to grow, and many improvements were completed. During a trying season, the pulpit was vacant for approximately two years; as a result, many members lost interest and selected to worship elsewhere. A few faithful members held fast to God's word and remained with the church. A request was made by the Deacons to Reverend Richard G. Dixon Jr. to preach the word to the remaining congregation.

Reverend Dixon honored the request and his name was submitted to the Pulpit Committee for Pastor immediately following Sunday service. The church accepted his name and Reverend Dixon accepted the position as Pastor.

The following also served as Pastor of the First Baptist Church: Reverend Rupert Paul, Reverend Dixon, Reverend Calvin R. Craven, Reverend James Thomas; Reverend Ronald Thomas (the son of Reverend James Thomas); Reverend James Thomas, Reverend Ronald Thomas, and Reverend Eddie Ware. After a season of various visiting ministers, Minister Larry J. Harris was called as Shepherd of the First Baptist Church by the pulpit committee.

The current pastor of the First Baptist Church is Pastor Michael G. Woods. This church has stood as a sentinel, pointing men, women and children towards heaven. It has served as a hospital for the sick, shelter for the homeless, a station for clothing the needy as well as a haven for those seeking knowledge of our Lord along with a place of rest. We will continue to stand on the promises of God, by being faithful, obedient and willing to learn.

We will continue to exercise our faith through fasting, praying and believing in God's words of "Upon this rock I will build My Church and the gates of hell shall not prevail against it."

May First Baptist Church continue to stand in years to come as its members represent a living monument of a savior who died so that all men might live.

Submitted by First Baptist Church, Lackawanna, New York

First Calvary Missionary Baptist Church
467 William Street
Buffalo, New York

In October 1972, a group of Christian believers associated by the covenant in the faith and fellowship of the gospel numbering seventy-eight met regarding the organization of the church. Our first aim was to form a mission, select a name, have three meetings, and form a corporation. The name selected was First Calvary Missionary Baptist Church, and our worship was held at 794 E. Delavan Avenue. On December 3, 1972, the church became incorporated.

Deacons Ulysses Norward, Zeddie Dennard, Clifton Yarbrough and Calvin Wilkins served as the first ordained deacons, who worked so faithfully and untiringly during this time.

On February 18, 1973, a meeting was called for the purpose of calling a pastor. This call was offered to and accepted by Minister Whitfield Washington, Jr. On May 5, 1973, a special meeting was called announcing that the church would be located at 50 Fillmore Avenue at Smith Street, which was offered to us for the sum of one dollar by the American Baptist Association. The first meeting was held at 50 Fillmore Avenue on September 2, 1973.

In two years, our membership doubled and God continued to shower his blessings upon us. Soon after we entered our new home, we began to make preparations to acquire property to build a more permanent structure. We purchased our first piece of property, 467 William Street in May 1975. Ten other pieces of property were subsequently purchased for the building of this edifice. In 1982, Groundbreaking ceremony was held for the building of our new edifice located at 467 William Street. The third Sunday of March 1985, we were blessed to march into our new home.

During the years between 1985 and 2007, many blessings came our way. Souls were added to the church, outreach ministry developed through teaching training, Sunday School, Baptist Training Union, Vacation Bible School, after school enrichment program, Elites, Serving With A Mission (S.W.A.M), Mission Ministry, Deaconess, Laymen, Usher Board, Nurses, Culinary, Pastor's Aid, Boy Scouts, Girl Scouts, Floral Club, Choirs and Youth Ministry.

After thirty-five years of service our beloved Pastor, Whitfield Washington, Jr. was called home on Friday, April 20, 2007. Remembering Pastor Washington's legacy we continued our mission of making disciples, and souls were added to the church. After three months of mourning, a pulpit committee was formed and began to work in September 2007. This committee worked untiringly for approximately one year in search for a pastor. Many days, weeks, and months were spent in prayer and fasting, waiting for God's revelation.

On Sunday, October 19, 2008, at a called meeting, God blessed us with Elder Jason J. Drayton. He began to serve as Interim Pastor on November 1, 2008. Nearly one year later on October 11, 2009 at a call meeting, Elder Jason J. Drayton became pastor. He has personally dedicated his life to strengthening the weak, encouraging the saints, and evangelizing the lost through preaching, teaching, discipleship, mentoring, counseling, and various other forms as God allows. Under his leadership, membership increased, ministries were restored and added to the church as "God advanced the kingdom as He saw fit."

First Shiloh Baptist Church
15 Pine Street
Buffalo, New York

The First Shiloh Baptist Church was established in the Ellicott district, known as the Fifth Ward, Ellicott District on October 1, 1916. The church grew out of an assembly of 12 persons who met in the home of Mrs. Hattie Causey at 25 Union Street for prayer meetings. The only known names of the group were Reverend Fredrick E. Edmunds, Walter Campbell, August Valentine, Nathan McCullough, Bert Leftwich, William Thompson, Sandy Thomas, Mrs. Minnie Fitzhugh, Mrs. Pearl Campbell and Mrs. Causey. The group chose as its pastor, The Reverend Fredrick Edmunds who was a member of the Michigan Avenue Baptist Church.

Pastor Edmunds succeeded in adding new members to the congregation, unfortunately after serving a mere eight months, dissatisfaction among the 77 members resulted in a split of the church. Pastor Edmunds remained with on faction, which called itself the First Shiloh Baptist Church. The other faction retained the name of Shiloh for a time but soon changed it to the Trinity Baptist Church.

The First Shiloh Baptist Church headed by Pastor Edmunds used as its new home, a storefront at 416 Clinton Street. Sunday

School classes were set up and officers selected Nathan McCullough as Superintendent. During 1917, the membership increased by 50 percent. To help meet the needs of newcomers to Buffalo who were migrating in great numbers from the south, the Willing Workers Club and the Missionary Society were formed. On November 13, 1917, the church was formally incorporated as the First Shiloh Baptist Church. In November 1918, the congregation 'called" The Reverend Elijah J. Echols, Sr. of Columbus, Mississippi. Pastor Echols accepted and began his pastorate of the First Shiloh, which would last more than forty years. In May 1921, the church congregation moved into the building at 40 Cedar Street. For the next forty-five years, this building was the home of the First Shiloh Baptist Church.

Much of what First Shiloh has become is due to the leadership and foundation provided by Reverend Elijah J. Echols Sr. During the more than four decades of Reverend Echols' pastorate, many ministers served Shiloh. Sons of Shiloh who were ordained into the ministry under Reverend Echols, Sr. were the Reverends Elijah J. Echols Jr., Walter M. Echols, George Bell, Ivor Moore, Spurgeon B. Donaldson, Phale D. Hale, M. Samuel Pinkston, William K. Richardson, Thomas J. Woodyard, James Robinson, Leo Murphy and F.D. Reid. All of these ministers serve or have served as successful pastors in churches across this country. On May 16, 1961, after serving for 43 years as pastor of First Shiloh, Reverend Elijah J. Echols Sr. passed away. Reverend Elijah Echols, Jr. was elected to succeed his father as pastor. Formal installation of Reverend Echols Jr. took place in March 1962.

The groundbreaking ceremonies for the current church building were held on August 9, 1964. On May 15, 1966, members and friends made the short trip of one block from the old building to the new $700,000 church structure, which was formally dedicated on July 3, 1966. During the 22 years of pastor Echols' able and dedicated leadership, First Shiloh remained strong and attained nationwide recognition as an outstanding church, especially within the black community. Under Pastor Echols' leadership First Shiloh continued with 27 boards, clubs and auxiliaries.

During his pastorate, not only did he save souls for Christ; he also made a tremendous impact on the local and regional ecumenical community. He served as President of the Board of directors of the Buffalo Area Council of Churches, and was President of the Empire State Baptist Convention at the time of his death. After the death of Pastor Echols, Jr., the church elected the Reverend Timothy Careathers of the First Baptist Church in Milford, Connecticut. He was installed as the fourth pastor on June 30, 1985. Reverend Careathers served approximately one and half years before resigning February 15, 1987.

On June 17, 1988 the congregation elected Reverend Leslie D. Braxton as its fifth pastor. Under pastor Braxton's leadership five persons were ordained and licensed to gospel ministry: John Ross Dixon, Kathi Chavous, Melvin Maxwell, Jannie Redmon and Kimberly Gladden. A total of thirteen deacons were ordained with Earline Oliver ordained as Shiloh's first female deacon.

During this period, the long awaited First Shiloh Housing Development Corporation came to fruition.

In 1998, the First Shiloh Christian High School opened as the first Afro-Centric Comprehensive Christian High School in the Buffalo, New York area. After a total of 13 years of service at First Shiloh, in August 1999, Dr. Braxton accepted the "call" from Mount Zion Baptist Church in Seattle, Washington.

In December 2000, the congregation elected Reverend Artis McKinley Royal as the sixth pastor of the First Shiloh Baptist Church. Pastor Royal implemented new church Mission and Vision statements, which set the tone for enhancing and creating new ministries. Building improvement projects were completed, which included remodeling the kitchen, baptistery, and other neglected areas of the edifice. The nursery environment and services were revitalized, and a new van was purchased to meet transportation needs. In August 2003, Pastor Royal accepted the call to shepherd the flock at Pilgrim's Rest Baptist Church in Memphis, Tennessee.

In October 2006, Reverend Jonathan R. Staples of Palo Alto, California accepted the congregation's call to be the seventh pastor. Pastor Staples is the former Senior Pastor of the Jerusalem Baptist Church of Palo Alto, CA. He holds a Bachelor's degree from Stanford University and a Masters of Divinity from Princeton. Additionally, he has completed all of the coursework for a Doctorate of Ministry from San Francisco Theological Seminary. Pastor Staples places high priorities on discipleship and growing people. He envisions the church as one that builds relations through preaching, praise, promoting fellowship and proclaiming the Gospel.

Submitted by First Shiloh Baptist Church

Free Spirit Baptist Church
62 Titus Avenue
Buffalo, New York

On Sunday, February 15, 1987, Reverend Timothy L. Careathers announced to the congregation of the First Shiloh Baptist Church, his intention to resign as Pastor. Later that day, shortly after worship service, 29 people met in the home of Deacon and Mrs. Joseph Jackson at 376 Martha Avenue, Buffalo, New York to share sentiments concerning Pastor Careathers' resignation. It was

during this time of sharing that everyone present expressed a strong interest in continuing to worship together. By the end of this meeting, a decision was made to organize a new church.

Later that week, on February 20, 1987, the 211 men, women, and children met at the St. Augustine Center to discuss the organization of a new church. The late Reverend L.T. Boyce, the pastor of Calvary Baptist Church, assisted in the organization of the church and gracefully offered an invitation to this group to worship with the congregation at Calvary Baptist Church that following Sunday, February 20, 1987. "Shake it Off" was the powerful sermon delivered by Pastor Careathers.

In order to facilitate the incorporation process, the members voted to name the church Free Spirit Missionary Baptist Church. Reverend Allen Stanley, President of the Empire State Convention and Reverend L.T. Boyce were instrumental in offering encouragement and advice for developing strategies for organizing. The organization process was divided into three integral components: Spiritual Development group, led by Deacon Joseph Jackson, was given the task of developing an order of worship, Sunday School and also played a major role in finding a place of worship. This group also developed a Bible Study and Prayer and Praise Service for Wednesday nights.

The Management Team, chaired by Sister Velma Williams, was given the task of developing a structure for the church by drafting by-laws and identifying persons to the Pastor that were willing to be in service to the church. The Finance and Accounting Group was led by Sister Louiza Hord and a budget and system of accounting was developed.

The first worship service conducted at the 1490 Jefferson Avenue site was held on March 1, 1987 and Reverend David Chisholm was the guest minister and Deacon Amos Banks was the presiding officer in charge of worship that Sunday. The Mass Choir sang praises; ushers provided hospitality and Sister Bessie Patterson and Sister Sharon Patterson were our first visitors.

During a meeting on March 29, 1987, Reverend Careathers was elected as Pastor of the Free Spirit Missionary Baptist Church. Brother Walter Kemp, Brother Dewayne Palmer, and Brother Lee Myree were accepted as trial deacons and Sister Ada Hall was identified as chairperson of the Trustee Board. Free Spirit Missionary Baptist Church continued to grow both spiritually and financially. In July of 1987, "Hand Me Another Brick" building campaign was started to secure funds for the mortgage for the church building located at 1242 Jefferson Avenue.

After three spiritual and financial prosperous years, Pastor Careathers resigned as Pastor. On Friday, January 26, 1990, Trustee Velma Williams received the resignation of Reverend Timothy Careathers. On Sunday, January 28, 1990, Reverend Arthur Boyd was elected as interim minister of Free Spirit Missionary Baptist Church.

On November 5, 1990, Reverend Al B. Sutton Jr., of Shiloh Baptist Church of Port Royal, Virginia, was elected pastor. Under his leadership, administrative changes were made and various ministries were developed. Through Reverend Sutton's leadership, Free Spirit's presence was being felt in the community. "Back to Africa" was a yearly celebration. Because of the growth of the ministries, by January 1994, Pastor Sutton and a "Transition Team", under the leadership of the late Brother William Gaiter, began the search for a larger place of worship. Through the efforts of many, the properties of 60-64 Titus Avenue, Buffalo, New York were purchased by the membership and on Sunday, July 24, 1994, the first worship service was held in the new location.

On the last Sunday of July 2001, Reverend Al B. Sutton, Jr., informed the congregation that he had been called to pastor the Sixth Avenue Baptist Church of Birmingham, Alabama. On August 13, 2000, Pastor Sutton delivered his farewell sermon. Before Pastor Sutton's departure, he offered a recommendation that Free Spirit Missionary Baptist Church leadership elect Reverend Anthony G. Harris to serve as interim minister.

After a long, tedious, and prayerful search, Reverend Anthony G. Harris was elected by the membership to become the Pastor of Free Spirit Missionary Baptist Church on December 16, 2001. Pastor Harris has demonstrated that he is a visionary and a pastor with a servant's heart.

The super-charged and high energy leadership style of Reverend Harris has provided the impetus required to help propel the ministry to higher dimensions. Plans are currently underway to develop a Bereavement Ministry, increasing Community Outreach, Reading and Computer Literacy Program, and Family Preservation and Empowerment Community Center. Technology has also been added to the administrative and financial offices of the ministry.

From this union of pastor and people, a "New Free Spirit", a spirit of love and unity has come. As we endeavor to equip the saints, evangelize the world, and worship God in spirit and truth, we covenant to continue to "Seek ye first the Kingdom of God; and all these things will be added unto us." (Matthew 6:33)

Submitted by Free Spirit Baptist Church

Friendship Baptist Church
402 Clinton Street
Buffalo, New York

Friendship Baptist Church was originally organized as an unincorporated Baptist religious organization sometime during the year of 1913. The church held services in the homes of its members. Little was preserved of the history of the church during this period of its initial organization until its reorganization in 1915, under the leadership of Reverend R.B. Robinson. He was considered to have been the first minister of Friendship.

Reverend R.B. Robinson was called in 1915 and served until his death in 1929. The church moved into its first permanent sanctuary located on the corner of Pratt and Clinton streets. Following the death of Reverend Robinson, Reverend Twilus Davis was called in April 1929. On January 30, 1930, Reverend Davis obtained the parcel of land located at 146 -- 148 Hickory St. near the corner of Clinton Street to be the site of the new sanctuary. The cornerstone was laid during 1931. Reverend Davis left Friendship in March 1938.

In 1939, the church called Reverend Major J. Jenkins of Memphis, Tennessee to serve as its third pastor. During his pastorate the church purchased a grocery store known as the Friendship Community Market and renovated the sanctuary. Reverend Jenkins passed away June 23, 1943.

Reverend Clarence L. Franklin was called in 1943 to serve as Friendship's fourth pastor. On May 26, 1944, the church purchased the parsonage at 179 Glenwood Avenue and began her radio ministry broadcast on Sunday mornings. Reverend Franklin left Friendship in 1946.

The church called Reverend Richard H. Dixon, Sr. to serve as its fifth pastor in 1946. By January 1, 1947, the mortgage debt had been retired and the building at 146 -- 148 Hickory St. was improved and renovated. In 1948, Reverend Dixon left Friendship and organized the Second Temple Baptist Church.

Reverend Edward D. McNeely was called to serve in 1948. On November 10, 1952 the church entered into a building contract for the present sanctuary. Ground was broken on June 7, 1953 and on August 7, 1954, following the parade and motorcade, we marched into the new sanctuary. The debt was retired in 1965. In 1967, the church sold the parsonage at 179 Glenwood Avenue and purchased property at 117 Humboldt Parkway. Reverend McNeely passed away on August 30, 1977.

Reverend A. Charles Ware was called in July 1978 to serve as the seventh pastor. During his pastorate our bus ministry was expanded, land for a parking lot was acquired, the sanctuary was renovated, a garage was built to house the church's vehicles, Friendship Manor was constructed, a lift-a-vator was installed and the Edward D. McNeely Education Building was completed. Reverend Ware passed away on July 21, 1998.

In August 1999, Reverend William S. Wilson, Jr. was called to serve as the eighth pastor. During his pastorate, he created Phat Saturday and Jamm with the Lamb. Reverend Wilson left Friendship in 2005.

Reverend Daris Dixon – Clark, a native of North Carolina, answered the call to serve as the ninth pastor of Friendship in January 2007. Reverend Clark is deeply committed to the church and the community as evidenced by his past membership in the Coalition of Urban Pastors of Syracuse, NAACP, and the Empire State Missionary Baptist Convention. Pastor Clark's goal for Friendship was to strengthen us as a unified body of Christ, as well as a strong leader within the Baptist community. Reverend Clark's personal mission is to glorify God through effective preaching and teaching of God's word and live a life that is the full expression of his God given gifts.

www.friendshipmissionarybc.org/

Friendship Missionary Baptist Church
5652 Saunders Settlement Road
Lockport, New York

In the fall of 1951, Friendship Missionary Baptist Church was organized by the late Deacon and Sister Essie Williams and a number of others. The nineteen Christian members began worshipping in a small building at the corner of Market and Mill Street in Lockport, New York. Within a year, the building at 5652 Saunders Settlement Road was purchased and the first service was held there in July 1952. God called the first pastor, J. S. Scott of Rochester, NY, who served the congregation for three years. Following Pastor Scott, God called T. L. Ransom to pastor Friendship. For nine years, he labored in the vineyard before being called to pastor Cedar Grove Baptist Church in Buffalo.

In 1963, the Lord sent Pastor James Gooden who served Friendship faithfully for thirty-four years. In 1997, he passed from labor to reward, but he will long be remembered. Under Pastor Gooden's leadership, Pastor Willie Montgomery was ordained and served as the assistant pastor. Also Minister Caleb Bell Sr. was licensed to preach and Deacons Clifford Porter and Jerry McClain were ordained.

Some improvements were made to the interior and exterior of the building; however, Pastor Gooden was taken by the Lord before his vision was fulfilled. After the death of Pastor Gooden, Minister Caleb Bell served as the interim pastor for ten months.

On November 1, 1998, the Lord sent Pastor Herman L. Potts to Friendship. Under his leadership and with God's blessings, the vision continues. Evangelist Gussie O'Steen was licensed on July 13, 2004 and ordained on June29, 2008.

Two deacons, the late LeTana Crenshaw and Robert Turner, were ordained and two others, James Floyd and Winston Jenkins, are in training. Additionally, improvements have been made to the Gooden Annex, the kitchen and dining room, a church van was purchased, and the sanctuary was painted and carpeted.

Friendship is blessed with Sister Classie Knight, one of the original members who is still laboring in the vineyard forty-eight years later. Truly God has blessed Friendship beyond measure and we praise God for all of His many blessings. The vision continues.

Submitted by Friendship Baptist Church, Lockport, NY

Gethsemane Baptist Church
55 Grape Street
Buffalo, New York

Gethsemane Baptist Church was organized on March 31, 1949 in Buffalo, New York. Reverend Henry B. Shaw, a founding member, served as the first pastor. Under his twelve year pastorship, the congregation grew and moved from 430 Broadway to 43 E. Utica Street. The church later moved to 1300 Jefferson Avenue. Reverend Shaw served as pastor until he was called home from his labor to rest on October 31, 1961. One year later on October 23, 1962, God brought us to our present location of 55 Grape Street.

On January 1, 1965, Reverend Herbert Vincent Reid was called to pastor Gethsemane Missionary Baptist Church. In 1962, by chance he was studying at Rochester's Colgate Divinity School, and he was invited at age twenty to be a guest preacher at Gethsemane because Pastor Shaw was ill. Reverend Reid returned to Gethsemane  after completing his studies and saw it grow into a large and well-known Baptist congregation.

Through the years, Gethsemane has become a rallying point for community progress and a center for freedom and justice. The Erie County Southern Christian Leadership Conference was born here, as well as the Black Leadership Forum, the Friday Lunch and Community Dialogue, the Interracial Task Force, Ministers Against Narcotics, and the Concerned Citizens Group.

Under Reverend Reid's leadership, the mortgage was burned on both the old and new building in 1975. The addition of a new sanctuary was completed in 1989. And on September 17, 1992, the groundbreaking was held for the Gethsemane Manor a senior citizen facility.

On November 23, 2008, the mortgage was burned on the new sanctuary. Reverend Tommy L. Babbs was ordained and licensed to the Gospel ministry. Deacons James Hicks, Leonard Troublefield, James Booker, Jr., John Wilson and David Hayes were ordained. Reverend Reid faithfully served God and his church for 47 years. On Thursday, November 27, 2008, God took Reverend Reid home to live with him for eternity. On December 27, 2008, Deacon James Booker Jr. asked for thirteen members from the congregation to serve on the Pulpit Search Committee: Deacons: James Booker Jr., David Hayes Sr. and John Wilson; Deaconess Joyce Doss; Trustees: Wilette Brown, Cynthia Compito, and Carla Martin; Mothers: Dolores Johnson, Lois Lynch, and Attrice Porter; Members: Lorraine Ballou- Bonner (Vice chair); Karen Peterson and Dawn E. Sanders (Chair), appointed by our late pastor.

As it is written in Jeremiah 23:4, God will *set up shepherds over them which shall feed them, and they shall fear no more, nor be dismayed, neither shall they be lacking.* On September 26, 2009, the Pulpit Search Committee conducted a vote for pastor and Reverend Frank Raines III was selected as our third pastor in the church's 61 year history. Under our Servant and Pastor Raines, the church has renovated and restructured the parsonage and executive wing, replaced the roof on the old sanctuary at a cost of $60,000 (a gift from God), consolidated offerings and instituted serving communion during morning worship, and led the review and audit of the finances. Also Gethsemane reenrolled in the National Convention and Congress of Christian Education. Pastor Raines became a member of the New Zion Missionary Baptist Church under the leadership of Reverend John Williams. Blessed with Pastor Raines' leadership, we prayerfully await greater direction from God.

Greater Apostolic House of Prayer
1455 Fillmore Avenue
Buffalo, New York

In 1979, a small group of saints, being inspired by God, was moved to fast and pray out of the need for a closer walk with God. The prayer and cries of God's people began to move him on the throne – as they prayed, they could hear in their spirit God saying, "If my people, which are called by my name, shall humble themselves, and pray, and seek my face, and turn from their wicked ways, then will I hear from heaven, and will forgive their sin, and will heal their land. "God began to bless this prayer group organized by Sister Jacqueline Foye.

At that time we met twice a month, and then God said, "That's not nearly enough." We then began to pray every Friday night at 12 o'clock a.m. The lateness of the hour was to accommodate those that were working second shift and not to interfere with any of our regularly scheduled services. Sister Foye requested of God that He inform the people about the prayer and He should send in those with a need and those knowing that He "heareth the prayers of the righteous."

God began to meet the needs of His people as they began to repent. Yokes were broken; many were healed both in body and spirit. He taught us how to forgive as the Scriptures has said not seven times, but seventy times seven. Know that when God began blessing the devil began messing. But we had an assurance that Christ would not fail us, and that "no weapon formed against us would prosper," and every tongue that rose against us in judgment we would condemn. For this is the heritage of the servants of God. We were under definite direction of God, being told when, where, and how to move. The Lord said on one occasion, "I will lead you out of your present place of worship, and charge the angels to prepare for you a building where you can pray continually, and daily shall I be your praise."

Deacon James Foye began looking for buildings in which we could convert into a church. Sister Pearl Martin, knowing of this endeavor, called the Pastor informing her of the availability of 1482 Fillmore Avenue, then the home of Brother and Sister Charles Fields, Jr.

For He desires to be praised with the sound of the trumpet, with dancing, with stringed instruments and organs, and loud cymbals, with high sounding cymbals. He demanded that everything that has breath praise Him. Praise ye the Lord! Jeremiah 3:15, "And I will give you pastors according to mine heart, which shall freed you with knowledge and understanding. "Acts 20:28," Take heed therefore unto yourselves, and to all the flock, over which the Holy Ghost hath made you overseers, to feed the church of God, which he hath purchased with his own blood." God fulfilled these two scriptures when He anointed, and then placed Sister Jacqueline Foye over this group as Pastor and overseer.

On Sunday, November 11, 1979, we held our first service at 211 Walden Avenue in the home of Evangelist Maryland Kelly Davis. There were eleven present. The number was small but the spirit of God was great. "For where two or three are gathered together in my name, there am I in the midst of them, saith the Lord." Our service was then moved to 396 Wyoming Avenue in the home of Pastor and Deacon Foye.

Even in our infancy, God blessed us with a choir, of about six Holy Ghost filled young people. Evangelist Valerie Foye, a very consecrated and talented young woman was asked by the pastor to train this group that they may sing unto the Lord a new song.

Knowing that "A man's gift maketh room for him, and bringeth him before great men." The six sounded like twelve while they sang and made melody in their hearts to God. Many were blessed, and received a message in song. Membership began to grow. The Foyes' living room was not large enough to hold the people that God sent. Backsliders began to return to God, families were reunited. We began to seek God more fervently for a place to worship.

Upon looking the house over, Deacon Foye was inspired by God that this was to be the new home of the Apostolic House of Prayer. The spirit of the Lord began to reveal every architectural plan to the Deacon that could only come from the Master Builder Himself.

God began to dictate from heaven every wall to be moved and every light switch to be replaced. The very first day of construction, Deacon Foye alone knocked down three walls with more pleasure and enjoyment and satisfaction than any bulldozer from Kulback Construction Company. He came home to his wife, our Pastor, dirty and dusty, but happy for at last he was building the church that had only existed in his heart because people said it couldn't be done. As the church began to materialize, the Saints began to organize themselves with the task of cleaning the debris, getting full of excitement and expectation. "For without a vision the people perish."

Sunday, twelve noon, February 10, 1980, we the members of the Apostolic House of Prayer embraced our God-given building. At this time we had a membership of twenty. The Lord blessed us with deacons, missionaries, and mothers, supplying us with everything that we needed the more we yielded ourselves to Him.

Sister Judith Brown Curuth was the first person to be baptized in Jesus' name and filled with the Holy Ghost in our new church. Then it was as if God said "sit back and watch me do it." He began to send families, people from all walks of life and of every profession. We purchased a Hammond organ, a baby grand piano, and a set of camber drums, all to enhance and enrich the service of God. God blessed us and put us on the map, giving us favor with people. We were on Brother Ted Johnson's Gospel Television Show (WKBW-TV Channel 7) on numerous occasions. God opened doors for us in the cities of Buffalo and Rochester New York, and in the states of New Jersey, Maryland, Michigan, Virginia, and the District of Columbia. As the writing of this history, we have a membership of one-hundred and twenty-five. Many that started out with us no longer walk with us. We have a pet saying here at the Apostolic House of Prayer "Hold on to your seat, for God is filling vacancies and adding to the church daily such as should be saved. The Lord is not slack concerning His promise, as some men count slackness, but is long-suffering toward us, not willing that any should perish, but that all should come to repentance."

We, the saints at the Apostolic House of Prayer, extend our thanks and deepest appreciation for having you join us in our "Building on Faith" program. For we believe as it is written, "Eyes have not seen, nor ears heard, neither have entered into the hearts of men the things which God has prepared for them that love Him."

We request the prayers of the righteous to continue praying for us. "For we are not ashamed of the gospel of Christ; for it is the power of God unto salvation to everyone that believeth... For if God be for us, who can be against us?" On the 11th day of November, 1992, the Apostolic House of Prayer had been established for 13 years. We are no longer that little church on Fillmore Avenue! Having gone through much toiling, laboring and buffeting – we feel that God considers us a powerhouse, a soul-saving station, a place of refuge, a fortified fortress for

Him! We have paid our dues, yet the blessings have been overwhelming! Our vision has not diminished in its intensity, but has continually grown.

Our former and existing church, which housed our humble beginnings, is the foundation of everything good that takes place at The Greater Apostolic House of Prayer. It is "God's Little People" (G.L.P.) Day Care Center, as well as an outreach program assisting the homeless and those with special needs.

Meanwhile, we are located directly across the street at 1455-1465 Fillmore Avenue on the corner of Woodlawn Avenue, where we continue to magnify and praise His name! The Pastor has heard from the Lord. His command was, "Take heed now, for I hath chosen thee to build a house for the sanctuary: be strong, and do it."

The Greater Apostolic House of Prayer
Church Family

Greater Faith Bible Tabernacle Church
391 Edison Avenue
Buffalo, New York

On December 15, 1981, Bishop and Sister Halton, who at that time resided at 54 Hamlin Road, opened their home for prayer service and Christian Fellowship. It was through this time of prayer and fellowship, that the inception of the Faith Bible Tabernacle Church was birthed by divine providence. For through these prayer services, God brought together a body of fellow believers, consisting of Bishop Nathan S. Halton, Sister Antoinette Halton, Eric Campbell, Jesse Evans, Dorothy Evans and Roberta Lockhart.

God placed within the hearts of these six God-fearing people, the same thought: To organize a church within the Buffalo Community. Their focal objective was as it is today, to reach out and help the lost for Jesus Christ! Our first Sunday Service was held on Sunday, December 21, 1981, at the Expressway YMCA, where Elder Halton had secured a room for worship. Our congregation began to expand and God in his infinite wisdom, lead Bishop Halton to the Immaculate Heart of Mary School, located at 391 Edison Avenue, in search for a place that could accommodate our expansion of worship services and growth.

On March 1, 1981, the Faith Bible Tabernacle Church began renting one classroom in the building of the Immaculate Heart of Mary School located at 391 Edison Avenue for Sunday and weekly services. For better than two years, this property was up for sale, and at that time, the asking price was out of our range. which included the retiring of the Head Priest of the parish and the closing of the Bingo Hall.

However, God began to work in our behalf, removing all obstacles. We continued to work together, and in September of 1985, we stepped out on faith, and began negotiations for the purchase of the building. We encountered many hardships and disappointments in our effort to finance the building with the lending institutions of the City of Buffalo. Despite our struggles, Bishop Halton and the congregation continued to believe God, and in July of 1986, God opened up doors for us which man had shut. The Catholic Diocese accepted our offer without any rebuttal, and told us of their willingness to hold the mortgage for a period of ten years. With one mind and one heart, we were determined to pay off this loan within three years. In August of 1989, our efforts were accomplished! Two months later, on Sunday, October 4, 1989, THE MORTGAGE WAS BURNED!

With this great feat being accomplished, our faith was fueled and we knew that the city of Buffalo was ours. Under the leadership of our pastor, we began knocking on new doors and watched them open unto us. These doors provided us with many opportunities to help meet the needs of the people. The Breath of Life Day Care Centers, the Breath of Life Media, and the Greater Faith Housing Corporation are just a few of the doors that were opened. They allowed us to follow our beloved pastor's philosophy, "Christians must be thermostats that change the climate and not thermometers that measure it."

On Saturday, May 27, 2006, our ministry suffered the greatest loss ever, when our beloved, Pastor, Founder and Father in the gospel was called home. We shall forever remember the lessons that he taught us and will use them to continue to enhance the lives of men and women everywhere. The legacy of Greater

Faith Bible Tabernacle Church continued as God sent us our new leader Pastor Darrell L. Fairer. On February 10, 2007, he was installed as Senior Pastor. He is committed to helping individuals find, function in and fulfill their God-given destiny.

God's Kingdom Church of Excellence where we are *Building People That Will Build the Kingdom Of God!*

Greater Hope Baptist Church
8 Verplank Street
Buffalo, New York

In 1949, the late Reverend John H. Monroe envisioned a church from whence the Gospel of Jesus Christ could go forth. Reverend Monroe, along with eight fellow laborers in the cause of Christ, organized the Greater Hope Baptist Church. The eight people at the Church's inception were Mrs. Georgia Pagues, Mrs. Margie Chandler, Mrs. Rowena Scott, Mr. Grover Darden, Mrs. Marie Goodwin, Mr. Anthony Gross, Mr. Millard Cook and Mrs. Sarah Cook. Greater Hope was first located at 600 Clinton Street. As the church grew there was a need for a larger building, so it relocated to 214 Clinton Street.

In 1959, Greater Hope moved to its present location. According to plans drawn up by Pastor Monroe, the building was remodeled, and the cornerstone was laid in 1970. Under Pastor Monroe's leadership, Greater Hope did great things for the Kingdom. In 1983, Pastor Monroe was called from labor to rest, leaving behind his faithful wife, Mrs. Amanda Monroe. After Pastor Monroe's death, Reverend John Pratcher served as interim pastor. With the aid of the church leadership, headed by Deacon Brantley, Greater Hope moved forward by "being like-minded, having the same love, being one in spirit and purpose."

In April 1984, Reverend James C. Blackburn Jr. was called to the pastorate of the church. Preceding his call to the pastorate of Greater Hope, under the leadership of the late Dr. S. W. Williams, Jr., he served as the co-pastor of the New Zion Institutional Missionary Baptist Church of Buffalo and the Greater Galilee Institutional Missionary Baptist Church of Indianapolis, Indiana.

Dr. Blackburn is foremost a minister of the Gospel, and since his arrival, our church has grown spiritually and physically. Under his pastoral leadership, several pieces of property have been purchased, and parking lots have been installed. The church building has been completely renovated.
The lower level was dedicated and named in memory of Reverend John H. Monroe, our founding pastor.

Greater Hope supports and sustains many ministries, notably, our television and radio programs, where the Sunday School lesson is presented and people are encouraged to go to church. Over the years, the faces of the congregation have changed, but the church's goals and aspirations remain bringing honor and glory to our Lord and Savior Jesus Christ.

As we look to the future, we look with confidence for we know, "We can do all things through Christ who strengthens us."

Dr. Blackburn is a Man of God, nevertheless, a man with a vision. The members of Greater Hope have taken encouragement from our Pastor's leadership. Dr. Blackburn's favorite sayings are "God has a way with promises. He keeps them," and "He that winneth souls is wise."

www.greaterhopebuffalo.org/

Greater Refuge Temple of Christ
943 Jefferson Avenue
Buffalo, New York

In 1937, Elder H. J. Spencer from the Church of Our Lord Jesus Christ in Columbus , Ohio came to Buffalo. He later sent a minister to start and pastor a new Church of Our Lord Jesus Christ in Buffalo, New York. Elder Spencer sent Elder William L. Booker to Buffalo, to pastor Refuge Temple Church which he pastored until he went home to be with the Lord in 1945. Bishop H. J. Spencer and Elder Howard Holtz served as supply pastors from 1945-1948.

In 1949, Bishop Nathaniel V. Jones was installed as pastor of the Refuge Temple of Christ, Buffalo, New York with his devoted wife, Missionary Mother Mattie V. Jones standing by his side. Bishop Jones retired in 1972, due to illness. In 1973, Bishop Alfred S. Powell, presiding Bishop of Westchester and WNY diocese, appointed Elder Robert Sanders as the new pastor of Refuge Temple of Christ, in Buffalo , New York .

Bishop Sanders extended his ministry beyond the church and

into the Erie County Home and Infirmary and behind prison walls at the Erie County Penitentiary, where he served as Chaplain. His vision for the area of Jefferson and High Street was to expand and occupy the entire block on which Refuge Temple stood, from Earl/High Streets to Jefferson. He saw the block filled with structures owned by Greater Refuge Temple, which would be used to further the Kingdom of God. In order to expand, eight parcels of land had to be acquired from residents or commercial owners. It would take fourteen years to complete this phase of the vision.

In 1974, Refuge Temple purchased the first of these lots. In 1975, the second lot was purchased and by 1985, the Lord blessed Refuge Temple to be able to purchase the last of the lots necessary to build the first phase of his vision.
The Refuge Temple Education and Cultural Center would minister to and meet the needs of the "total person" (spiritually, mentally, physically and emotionally).

On August 21, 1983, Elder Sanders was consecrated Bishop by the Church of Our Lord Jesus Christ, to serve over the Western New York and Canadian Diocese. Construction of the Education and Cultural Center began in August 1986, and completed within seven months. Funds to begin this project were donated by members and friends of Refuge Temple. Bishop Sanders served as the general overseer of this project, which saved thousands of dollars. Members of the church voluntarily completed painting, cleaning, and finishing touches. In March 1987, the Center was completed and dedicated to the Lord for His service.

Bishop Bonner along with many elected officials, ministers, community members, members and friends of the church came to the Dedication Service. All guests had beautiful and encouraging words to say about the Center that houses the Refuge Temple of Christ Bible Institute. Office space, counseling rooms, a multi-purpose recreational room, and a fully equipped kitchen facility are also included in the Center. Upon completion of the Education and Cultural Center, many programs were initiated: blood pressure screening, summer lunch program, workshops for career planning, nutrition and diet workshops, adult literacy, and recreation for all ages and others. Realizing that our youth faced many challenges and problems, the first programs to be implemented was a tutorial/recreation program for school-aged youth.

Spiritually, the Refuge Temple Bible Institute, which is largely attended by non-members of the Church of our Lord Jesus Christ, is providing teaching and instruction in the Word of God.

Socially, the Center provides a place for both our youth and adults to mingle, share with other and play games and sports. Economically, the Center will assist by providing food and clothing for those who are in need. Legal and medical assistance is offered when needed.

The terrific response to the Word of God, while worship was going on, filled the sanctuary to capacity each Sunday morning. Chairs were placed in the aisles, and on some occasions people had to remain in the vestibule. The need to hear the truth from God's Word as it relates to the urgency of the times in which we live, and the soon coming of our Lord and Savior, Jesus Christ, have become first and foremost in the minds of the Saints of God.

Bishop Sanders, having heard from heaven about the next phase of the vision, knew that in order to move forward to bigger and better things, we needed to burn the Mortgage for the building of the Multi-purpose Hall and Education and Cultural Center. Bishop told the congregation that it would take faith, sacrifice and dedication to complete this task. He taught us that if we had the desire to contribute, God would give us the means.

With the theme: "We Can Do It Together" and the creation of the Attack Team, headed by Elder Gordon Sweat, (meaning we will attack this debt), all auxiliaries, groups, committees, and the entire congregation worked together to complete this task. To raise funds for the elimination of the mortgage, members and friends purchased plaques to be printed a name and favorite scripture.

Bishop Sanders is an anointed preacher and teacher of God's word. The ministry of Bishop Sanders is to reach the "total person." Under the dynamic leadership of Bishop Sanders, many positive and encouraging changes have been made at Greater Refuge Temple and the surrounding community. Bishop Sanders is a man of vision who realizes that he must be busy about God's business. He is an anointed speaker and author who has conducted and coordinated conferences, workshops and seminars enhancing spiritual growth and development.

As God's word goes forth from Bishop Sanders through the airways by radio, television and the pulpit, people from all over the city and surrounding areas have become a part of the Greater Refuge Family. One of Bishop Sander's visions that has been fulfilled is the beautiful new worship and praise center.

This sanctuary seats approximately 1000 people and everything in the sanctuary has a biblical significance. Another vision has become a reality—The Family Life Center. It provides a positive atmosphere and brings families together in a supportive and safe environment.

We are also grateful for the Christian Academy that is housed at the Greater Refuge Temple Complex. Located just a couple blocks away is the Citadel of Hope. This site gives young men hope that were hopeless and without a future. Another area for children is God's Little Children Child Development Center. This center will not be just another daycare but a learning center. Also Greater Refuge Temple Plaza houses a number of businesses on Jefferson Avenue.

As Greater Refuge Temple continues in its quest to be a church that makes a difference, we thank God for a man of vision and leadership such as Bishop Robert L. Sanders. To God Be the Glory!

www.grt.org

Hopewell Baptist Church
1301 Fillmore Avenue
Buffalo, New York

Hopewell Baptist Church was organized in the home of our founder and first pastor, the late Reverend John F.D. Lyles in January 1956 at 474 Genesee Street, Buffalo, New York. Attending ministers were the late Reverend J.B. Williamson, the late Reverend John Washington, the late Reverend James Lee, and the late Reverend Crockett.

The church was organized with eight members and we are blessed to still have two of them in our midst: Mother Marguerite Dunford and Mother Gladys Bonner. Pastor Lyles served faithfully until his death on December 8, 1987. He left us a legacy of "Love and Sharing." He worked tirelessly and hard to build up our church. He believed that a church is built on teaching, love, sharing and fellowship.

In June 1988, the Reverend Dennis Lee Jr. was called to be the pastor. Under his leadership and the vision that the Lord has given him, we have continued to grow both spiritually and physically. Blessed with constant growth, Hopewell moved from various locations throughout the city of Buffalo. In 1972, the Hopewell Baptist Church purchased and moved to 1307 Fillmore Avenue where we remained for thirty-two years.

In 1996, Pastor Lee shared with the congregation his vision of new church edifice and beseeched the Lord to allow us to purchase the land and build a new church edifice. By much prayer, the studying of God's Word and believing not just in

God but believing God every step of the way and doing it God's way through tithes and offerings, God allowed this vision to become a reality. Our new edifice at 1301 Fillmore Avenue was completed and we marched in and held our first worship service on October 9, 2004.

Here at the Hopewell Baptist, we too, like the Apostle Paul are still pressing toward the mark for the prize of the high calling of God in Christ Jesus.

www.hopewellbuffalo.org

Humboldt Parkway Baptist Church
790 Humboldt Parkway
Buffalo, New York

During the ministry of Elisha Tucker pastor of the Washington Street Baptist Church was called to organize a colored church to be constituted of the members of Washington Street Baptist Church. In the fall of 1836, 13 men and women withdrew From Washington Street Baptist Church and founded a second church of Buffalo, New York. This was the first group sent out on the mother church and in 1839 it was organized as the Michigan Street church. Later it was named Michigan Avenue, Baptist Church. This faithful band worshiped in a small wooden building then located at Niagara and Eagle Streets.

During that time due to the limited number of ordained African-American ministers living in the North, it was not uncommon for congregation of one ethnic group to be pastored by a minister of another ethnic background. Reverend William Monroe an ordained African-American minister was the first pastor. He served as pastor, teacher, janitor, and friend, and he rendered faithful service for 2 to 3 years. The second and third ministers, both Caucasian, were Mr. Verunder and Reverend Jeffrey. The church sent delegates in 1841 to the Baptist Association's annual session, and among them were Reverend Stephen Dutton, an ordained African-American minister from Toronto, Ontario. Reverend Dutton became the fourth pastor of the Second Baptist church in 1942.

The fifth pastor, Reverend Sharp, was Caucasian. Reverend Sharp traveled to England to raise money to build the house of worship in Buffalo. He was successful in his mission and the land for the building was purchased. Reverend Jeffries, an African-American minister, from Geneva, New York became the sixth pastor.

In 1841, Deacon William Quarles and Payton Harris, a grandfather of William Talbert, were delegates to the Baptist Association. Deacon Harris was considered a comparatively wealthy Negro of that historical period. He secured the bricks and materials used in the construction of the church building at 511 Michigan Avenue in 1844, Reverend Samuel Davis became the seventh pastor. Reverend Davis was a brick mason by trade. He labored long and hard with his hands and began to erect the building at 511 Michigan Avenue without being paid for his services. He also labored with his heart and mind to build up the kingdom of God. In 1845, under the leadership of Reverend Davis, the cornerstone was laid. Reverend Levi Tucker, pastor of first Baptist Church, and all the pastors from the Baptist Association along with representatives from their congregations took part in the cornerstone laying ceremony.

In 1848, the church had a membership of 81, and the Sunday school was organized to teach God's word. However in early 1849, the congregation was still worshiping in the basement because there were insufficient funds to finish the auditorium. After much prayer and planning, it was decided that each member should rent the pew at the cost of $10 per year. In this manner, the indebtedness was finally paid off and in late 1849 the building was dedicated. The building and lot cost approximately six thousand dollars.

The name of the church was changed from the second Baptist Church to The Michigan Avenue, Baptist Church. During the days of slavery in this country, the church maintained an underground railroad station where a great number of runaway slaves were cared for and helped to escape to Canada.

By 1885, the membership of the Michigan Avenue Baptist Church had been reduced to 13: eleven women and two men. The church joined the Buffalo Baptist Union and transferred the title of its property to the Union by mutual agreement. The union contributed extensive repairs to the building.

Eight pastors came in rapid succession until 1886 when Reverend Holland Powell came from Virginia and served for four years. In 1890, Reverend R. C. Quarles was called and served for two years. In 1892, Reverend J. Edward Nash came from Wayland Seminary (now Virginia Union) to Buffalo. He entered upon a ministerial career that resulted in 61 years of faithful service as pastor of The Michigan Avenue Baptist Church. The membership grew from 34 members in 1892 to about 400.

In 1912, Virginia Union University conferred an honorary degree of Doctor of Divinity upon Reverend Nash. In 1918, Reverend James Gant was called to serve as assistant pastor to Reverend Nash. He later continued in this role under Reverend Porter W. Phillips, the successor to Reverend Nash. Reverend Gant served the church faithfully from 1918 until his death in 1970. Reverend Dr. Nash retired as pastor in 1953 and received the distinguished honor of being named pastor emeritus of The Michigan Avenue, Baptist Church for life. A recognition banquet was held in his honor at the Michigan Avenue YMCA.

On November 8, 1953, Reverend Porter W. Phillips Jr. of Pittsburgh, Pennsylvania became pastor of The Michigan Avenue, Baptist Church. Reverend Phillips was a graduate of Union theological seminary where he had received the degree of bachelor of Divinity. Under the competent and capable leadership of Reverend Phillips, the church grew in membership, and financial strength, and in its total program. It became necessary to hold two worship services in order to accommodate the growing congregation.

Recognizing the inadequacy of the building at 511 Michigan Avenue, the congregation voted to purchase the Humboldt

Parkway Methodist Church and parsonage at 790 Humboldt Parkway in 1960. The church held a victory celebration from March 4 to March 26, 1960. The theme for the celebration was *Onward by the Grace of God.* A closing victory banquet completed the festivities.

Under Reverend Phillips' leadership, the congregation continued to increase in size over the next 19 years. During that time Reverend Davis served as executive assistant to Reverend Phillips. After 19 years of faithful service as pastor, Reverend Phillips resigned to accept the position of Executive Director of the Gladden Community House in Columbus, Ohio. He preached his farewell sermon in Buffalo at the 11 o'clock service on Sunday, September 24, 1972. The church sponsored a Circle of Friends banquet in his honor at the Holiday Inn at 620 Delaware Avenue that same evening.

In October 1972, Reverend John T. Hilliard was elected to serve as interim pastor. In December of 1972, the congregation voted to engage Reverend Hilliard as pastor. A native of Buffalo, he received his formal education here and graduated from Houghton college with a BS degree in Bible. In 1971, he received the MS degree in school administration at the State University College at Buffalo.

Reverend Hilliard brought capable leadership to Humboldt Parkway Baptist Church. He immediately launched the congregation on an $85,000 building improvement drive and encouraged the members to become tithers. Under his leadership the mortgage was burned in 1985. Since that time more than $200,000 in remodeling and renovation of the church building has been completed.

Both Reverend J. Daryl Wood and the late Reverend James L. Spencer served as assistant pastors under Reverend Hilliard. Reverend Robert Jackson was licensed by the church to preach the gospel and currently serves as associate Minister. Minister Alton Bowens also has been licensed by the church to preach the gospel. Reverend Hilliard's approach and example for the church has been to expound the stewardship of life. His emphasis has been on the church as a family and he has taught the members to express caring concern for one another.

The church has caught the vision of St. Matthew 25:34 – 40: I was hungry and you gave me meat; I was thirsty and you gave me water; I was a stranger and you invited me into your homes; naked and you clothed me; sick and in prison and you visited me...The church's mission is to give a helping hand to our community as we share our personal relationship with Christ.

We are taught to demonstrate his teachings in the way we live. We also share our Christian relationship by giving extensive support to home and foreign missions. Praise God as we remember our past and prepared to celebrate our future.

Note: The early church history of The Michigan Avenue Baptist Church was written by the late Mrs. Mary B. Talbert in 1908. This information was given to her by Mrs. Emerline Coy, a faithful member of the church for over 58 years. Credit is also given to Mrs. Rhoda Townsend, Mrs. Alma Brooks, and Mrs. Marguerite Nolan (church clerk for 56 years) for information added to our church history.

Submitted by Humboldt Baptist Church

Jordan Grove Baptist Church
1264 Kensington Avenue
Buffalo, New York

U pon this rock I will build my church and the gates of Hell shall not prevail against it. Matthew 16:18. Go ye therefore and teach all nations, baptizing them in the name of the father and of the son and of the Holy Ghost; teaching them to observe all things whatsoever I have commanded you, and Lo I am with you always, even unto the end of the world. Matthew 28:19-20.

With the blessed assurance of the first scripture and obeying the command of the second, six people became charter members of Jordan Grove Baptist Church: Reverend Henry Ford, Brother and Sister Alfonzo and Hazel Davis, Reverend and Sister John and Sylvia Oliver and Sister Beatrice Fields. They met and organized this church in the home of Brother and Sister Alfonzo Davis at 211 E. Utica Street, Buffalo, NY, on March 23, 1955. Reverend Henry Ford was elected pastor, Beatrice

Fields, secretary, and Brother Alfonzo Davis was appointed to serve as a deacon.

At this meeting, Sister Julia Oliver submitted the name *Jordan Grove Missionary Baptist Church* in honor of her home church in Brunswick, Georgia. The name was unanimously approved. Sister Hazel Davis, who was an aggressive and courageous Christian mother and her husband, Brother Alfonso Davis, were instrumental in securing our first church site at 170 Woodlawn Avenue. The landlord, Mr. Cooper, said he would not rent any portion of this building to a church; however, Almighty God troubled him in a dream, then Mr. Cooper gladly rented it to us. With thanksgiving, praise and adoration to our heavenly Father, we had our first worship services there on Sunday, April 17, 1955. Soon thereafter, Pastor Ford's own church, Calvary Baptist Church, the late Reverend Peter Trammell, pastor, conducted our church recognition and pastor's installation services. Subsequently, we bought the entire building from Mr. Cooper.

Under Pastor Ford's leadership, the church grew and progressed tremendously by the grace of God. Through Pastor Ford's profound teaching and preaching, quiet, persuasive, loving leadership, and through soul saving campaigns and revivals, souls were indeed converted to Jesus Christ. We thank God for the tremendous strides we made during his administration. We became a corporate body in 1960. Pastor Henry Ford led us from March 23, 1955 to April 1964 when he moved to California.

On September 15, 1964, we elected Reverend Glenn H. DuBois as pastor. He had previously served as Reverend Ford's assistant for about eight years. Pastor DuBois was also the first chairman of our deacon board. Pastor DuBois continued to lead us to higher heights of Christianity. He emphasized total stewardship, generous and joyful use of our time, talent and resources to the glory of God. He led us toward accepting God's plan for financing the church: tithes and offerings. Malachi 3:15, and continually reminded us that the principle of stewardship is not a gimmick for raising money, but a method for raising Christians.

We remained at 170 Woodlawn for 15 years, from April17, 1955 until March 29, 1970, when we had our sunrise services at 70 Woodlawn Avenue and our 11 a.m. worship at our new location, 106 Humboldt Pkwy, corner of Woodward Avenue. On Easter Sunday, April 14, 1974, we burned our mortgage for the 106 Humboldt site. We remained there for 16 1/2 years, from March 29, 1972 to December 21, 1980. For one month, we were temporarily located at 319 Northland Avenue while facilitating the move to 1264 Kensington Avenue. This site was also secured by the grace of God through the inspiration of our First Lady Emeritus, Sister Lurie L. DuBois, the insight of Pastor DuBois and the cooperation of our associate ministers, officers, and entire church membership.

On Sunday, January 25, 1987, we had a videotaped motorcade procession from 106 Humboldt Parkway to our present home. We entered our new building for our glorious morning worship services debt free. No mortgage. Praise God!

On Sunday, March 6, 1977, we began our radio ministry, a live one-hour Sunday service broadcast and continued for 12 years until 1989. During these 56 years, our church has licensed 25 preachers and ordained eleven. Nine of those became pastors: the late pastor Glenn Harvey DuBois, the late Pastor William Holley, Jr., Reverend George W. DuBois, Reverend Dr. Johnny Ray Youngblood, Reverend Leroy Adams, Jr., Reverend Dr. Kenneth Cox, Reverend Dr. Tony Matthews, Pastor C. C. Cox, Jr. and Reverend James L. Spencer, Jr.

God blessed us to progress exceedingly under Pastor DuBois' leadership from September 15, 1964 until He called Pastor DuBois on February 9, 2005 after 40 1/2 years of pastoral service. Under the leadership of Pastor DuBois, Jordan Grove moved twice, each of the buildings possessing the necessity of a growing congregation. Three church building mortgages were liquidated/burned and the third sanctuary purchased. The renovation and building project at our present location marks a pivotal place in our church history. It was our first major building project. We've expanded our sanctuary, pulpit and choir areas. We also added additional conference, office, and kitchen space and provided first-floor facilities and provisions for the handicapped. God blessed us to complete the church extension and renovations including the addition of air conditioning without a mortgage, a $135,000 project. To God be all the glory!

Pastor DuBois led the Upper Room Prayer Band in our annual ministry to the Erie County Home and Infirmary each New Year's Day for almost 50 years. This ministry which was started by the late Reverend Henry Hall was a yearly mission of love and caring. Messages of comfort and cheer were delivered throughout the facility with Christmas caroling, fervent praying, distribution of the choicest fruit and other forms of missionary outreach. It was amended to include the1490 senior citizens in the Grace Manor Nursing Home which was the first black owned and operated facility of its kind in the Buffalo area.

In 1993, we met Reverend Daniel Geply, a native of war torn Monrovia, Liberia, West Africa and pastor of Hope Temple Church there. Upon learning about the plight of the people in the homeland, Pastor DuBois was moved compassionately to encourage Jordan Grove to financially assist in sponsoring an orphanage and widows' home established in Monrovia by Pastor Geply. This assistance continues today under Pastor Cox's leadership and is the primary source of food and revenue for its residents and the surrounding community members.

Quarterly provisions of rice and money are sent to Monrovia. In 1996, the facility was officially named the Lurie L. DuBois Post War Orphanage Abandoned Children International Ministry, Inc. in honor of our first lady emeritus.

Pastor DuBois believed in continuous church growth which is evidenced by the multitudinous projects initiated, planned and executed under his direct leadership and guidance. The final major project he began was our church parking lot. It was his sincere desire that Jordan Grove have an off street parking area for members and visitors to safely park their vehicles while attending church activities. Toward this end we purchased property at 1240-1244 Kensington Avenue including a lot and church parsonage. Before God called Pastor DuBois home, we had completed the city of Buffalo's strenuous legal processes and secured the proper permits to go forward with the parking lot.

We elected our present pastor, Pastor C. C. Cox Jr. on April 14, 2005. Pastor Cox continues on the firm foundations laid by the late Pastor Henry Ford and the late Pastor Glenn H. DuBois. Pastor Cox led us to complete the parking lot project and we thank God. Under Pastor Cox's leadership, we have had a new roof placed on our church building, installed glass block windows in the front of our sanctuary, installed new doors, completed extensive needed plumbing work, purchased the new church van and installed security systems in our church parsonage. We thank God for these 56 years of service here at Jordan Grove.

Only three pastors have served us and all of them were brothers- in- law. We have witnessed the hand of God moving on our behalf down through the years, and we keep praying for the unity of Jordan Grove. Behold how good and how pleasant it is for brethren dwell together in unity, Psalm 113:1.

To God be all the glory!

Submitted by Lurie DuBois

Lincoln Memorial United Methodist Church
641 Masten Avenue
Buffalo, New York

For I know the plans I have for you," declares the Lord.." Jeremiah. 29:11

What someday would become Lincoln Memorial United Methodist Church began with prayer meetings led by the Reverend George C. Hollis and attended by several families in the home of Mr. and Mrs. Sylvester York at 484 Sycamore Street in late 1921, early 1922. By 1923, the growing group of worshippers found it necessary to move to larger quarters in the basement of Grace Methodist Episcopal Church at Michigan and North Division with its choir, ladies' aid and a young people's league, forerunner of the Methodist Youth Fellowship (MYF).In 1924, Reverend William R.A. Palmer of the Delaware Conference was appointed official pastor of this worshipping group which was, by then, called Grace Methodist Episcopal Mission. In the fall of 1925, the  small congregation was incorporated as part of the Genesee Conference and was moved to the property on Monroe and Howard Streets. An eventful march to the new church home on a beautiful Sunday marked the occasion.

Grace Methodist Episcopal Mission, was incorporated in the Genesee Conference in 1925, and for 17 years, was designated an official missionary and church extension project of the

Conference. Reverend William Palmer was their first official pastor, and the congregation became known as Lincoln Memorial Methodist Episcopal Church.

Among the founding families were the Yorks whose descendants include Madeline Anderson, Anna Evans, Geneva Herndon, Willie Evans; the Houses, whose descendants include Maude Dorsey, Jessie Roberts, Willie Dorsey; Arthur and Caroline Williams; the James Robinsons whose descendants include the Currys; the Tillman brothers; the Mays; the Blacks; the Burns; the Moores; the Channels and the Simmons. The records of the Trustees and Official Board members, as it was called, list Joseph Spencer, Evans House, Frank Moore, George Smith, Dora Thorton, Sylvester York and Minnie Walker, the first woman trustee.

In 1928, Lincoln Memorial celebrated its 5th Anniversary. By then, the church boasted a choir, Minister's Council, Church School, the Epworth League, a children's sewing class and included in its celebration activities Boy Scout night, a Buffalo

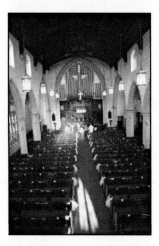

District supper, Young People's Night, Choir Night, Children's Hour, Women's Service, Men's Service and a masquerade party. The young congregation was off to a good start, blessed with dedicated and hard-working members and the desire to praise God in an organized fashion.

In 1929, Reverend Palmer was replaced by the Reverend William H. Horner as pastor. Throughout the ensuing years that spanned four decades, Lincoln became well established in the community, well respected in the Genesee Conference and by fellow Methodist Episcopalians.

Under Mrs. Horner, the daughter of the late Dr. Charles Tinley, renowned author of many of the hymns we sing even now, the choir grew in stature and reputation. She was known throughout the area and the state for her choral arrangements and musical plays. Some of her musical arrangements are still being used today. She worked very diligently with the Sunday School and the Children's Division, and hardly a child in the church or in the school across the street on Monroe (School 75), escaped her eye or her musical genius as each holiday was an occasion for a play or pageant. In 1953, Lincoln Memorial purchased its present spiritual home at Masten Street and Northland Avenue, then occupied by Trinity Methodist Episcopal Church.

And thus, on another historic occasion on July 4, 1954, Reverend Homer moved the Lincoln congregation to its new location as co-tenants for seven months with Trinity Church. His illustrious ministry lasted for 36 years until 1965.

In 1968, all Methodist Episcopal churches became United Methodist churches. The pastor who followed Reverend Homer was the late Reverend Willard A. Williams in 1966. He was considered a community builder, who created the Office of the Black Community Developer, a new church library, preparatory classes for new members and sought, in general to make our programs more relevant to the members as well as to the community.

The late Reverend Edmund Millet followed in 1970 with emphasis on strengthening laity ministries and initiated the church's first newsletter —FOCUS. Our major women's groups were organized into "circles" to provide diverse programs and ministries.

His ministry emphasized full church participation and involvement: basketball teams for youth, bowling leagues, Cub Scouts, sewing classes, a day care center.

Reverend Walter Barton succeeded Reverend Millet in 1978, followed by Reverend Melba Chaney in 1986; the late Reverend Dr. James Webb in 1996; Reverend Ewart Morris in 2002, the late Reverend Alicia Blake in 2006, and our current pastor, Reverend Patricia Brown who has served Lincoln since 2008.

From our beginnings in 1923, God has continued to bless this humble congregation with growth and discernment. We now have a Gospel choir, an early Praise Service, a Summer Enrichment Program for children, a Summer Vacation Bible School program, an After School Program (until 2010) - a collaborative effort with the public schools and Canisius College, to mention a few of our ministries. Through our missional outreach we support and assist the Central Center Café on the city's east side and the Asbury Shalom Zone on the west side. We have been blessed by God who has made us stewards of a beautiful facility sought by groups and individuals for weddings and other events. Lincoln Memorial United Methodist Church, as we celebrate 87 years of "Christ within Us" continues to add milestones to our legacy.

Mission Statement: The Lincoln Memorial United Methodist Church is an expression of Christ-like love, spreading the Gospel through Christ-like ministries to make disciples of Jesus Christ through acts of kindness, experiences of spiritual growth, worship, Christian teaching, missions and outreach.

History and photos submitted by Lincoln Memorial

Lutheran Church of Our Savior
30 Brunswick Boulevard
Buffalo, New York

The Lutheran Church of Our Savior, a Missouri Synod affiliate, has served the Buffalo community for more than 84 years. During its existence, the church has held services in three different locations, has been served by eight pastors, and has grown from an initial group of twelve (12) congregants to its present size of approximately 150 families.

The church began as a mission through the efforts of Mr. Chester Robinson. On January 1, 1926, the first services were conducted by Reverend Henry F. Wind, of the Lutheran Institutional Missions, in the home of Mr. and Mrs. James Washington, Sr. at 1424 Jefferson Avenue, corner of Woodlawn Avenue.

The Sunday School was begun at the same time. Among the eight children who attended these first Sunday School classes were the four Powell children, the late Kydson, Jr. the late Marion ("Sis"), Howard ("Buddy"), and Margaret (now Martin). They later would become Sunday School Superintendent (Kydson, Jr.), Deacon and Property Board Chair (Marion), and Treasurer-Historian (Howard). At the time the predominately

African American church was begun, the city's approximately 4500 African Americans totaled less than one percent of its population. Segregation was accepted in every branch of the city's social, economic, and political life. The nearest churches available to African Americans were two miles away in downtown Buffalo.

On October 31, 1931, with the assistance of area Lutheran churches, property at 94-96 Northland Avenue was purchased for the congregation.

The congregation had grown to sixty-one members. A 150-seat church was built. The Reverend Edward R. Pflug, who had been instrumental in acquiring the property, was installed as the first pastor on October 6, 1929. He served until 1938. By the late 1940s, the membership had increased to the point that two services were necessary each Sunday. The church conducted Saturday school, vacation bible school, and also Released Time Religious School for children who were released from public school one afternoon each week to attend religious instruction. Organizations in the church were the Ladies Aid Society (now Women's Guild), Young People's Society (now Youth Board), Men's Club, Deacon Board, Choir, Board for Christian Education and the Church Council.

On April 3, 1949, the Reverend Harvey J. Lehman was installed as the fourth pastor of the church. He was the first African American to serve the predominantly African American congregation. By 1956, the church on Northland Avenue had become too small for the congregation. In 1960, Trinity Old Lutheran Church, a German congregation at 26 Brunswick Boulevard, relocated to Sheridan Drive in the suburbs. The Lutheran Church of Our Savior purchased the property and moved to its present location. The church is located within Hamlin Park, a community that has been awarded historic designation by the Common Council of the City of Buffalo. The designation was awarded because of the community's park-like setting, interesting architecture, and numerous prominent African American residents, many of who had been active in government and civic organizations. By 1960, Buffalo's African American population had grown to 70,000. The Hamlin Park community was transitioning from German and Jewish to African American residents. It remained solidly middle class.

When the church was founded, members lived in the neighborhood and walked to church. Today, about ten percent of the families live in the surrounding suburbs. The church burned its mortgage in 1988. Despite vicissitudes caused by pastoral vacancies, the city's population losses, and fluctuations in membership, the ministry continues to thrive under strong and dedicated lay leadership developed under long serving ministers, Reverend Harvey Lehman (1949-1965) and Reverend Robert H. Wilson, Jr. (1967-1986).

A number of the early members are still pillars of the church: Howard Kydson Powell, Margaret Powell Martin, and Carmen Hare Harris. The church continues to be a meeting place for the community. Some of the activities of the church today that differ from those of the early church are praise dance groups, line dance parties, skating parties, and sleepovers.

As we enter the 21st century, advances in technology have influenced how members communicate. Computers facilitate communication by electronic mail, web pages, and social media networks such as Facebook.com, and Twitter.com. Almost everyone, including children, has a cell phone. Cameras are digital, i.e., they capture images on media cards instead of film, and action can be recorded on video cameras. Bible stories can be presented by PowerPoint.

Notwithstanding technological advances, the mission of the church remains the same-- to teach the Gospel-- and we strive to produce the next generation of church leaders.

I can do all things through Christ who strengthens me.
Philippians 4:13.

Submitted by Reva W. Betha

Macedonia Baptist Church
237 East North Street
Buffalo, New York

There was not a church in the Depew and Lancaster area, and so it was that Macedonia started out as a Missionary Circle in 1921 with the help of the late Sister Rosie Johnson and Sister Jenkins. The Melvin Company let them use a house on Livingston Avenue in Lancaster, NY, where they met until 1928, when the church was organized with the help of the late Deacon Charles Miner, who was the first deacon of the church. Then the church's name was New Hope Baptist Church.

In 1929, the late Reverend Joshua Hamilton was called as pastor and served for one year. The church moved to 27 Lavaret Street, Depew,  NY in 1930 where Reverend Eddie Wilkerson served as pastor. He served until he resigned in 1934. The church was without a pastor until August 1935, when Reverend A.A. Merriweather was called. In 1941, the church moved from Depew, NY to 468 Jefferson Avenue in Buffalo, NY. Since there was another church in the area named New Hope Baptist Church, and with the consent of the members, the name was changed to Macedonia Baptist Church, which was suggested by the late Deacon Miner. Two years later, 557 Jefferson Avenue was purchased.

In 1954, the church mourned the death of Pastor A.A. Merriweather. Following his successor's death, Reverend A. Stallworth was called as pastor and served from 1955 until 1960.

A fire at 557 Jefferson Ave in 1961 caused services to be relocated to Emmanuel Temple on Adam and Peckham Streets until 511 Michigan Avenue, the Michigan Avenue Baptist Church site, was purchased.

The church was recognized as a historical landmark in February 1973, because it had served as an underground railway for slaves entering into Canada.
From 1962-1964, Reverend J. H. Sanders served as pastor. Reverend Thomas J. Merriweather was called as pastor in October 1964. During his tenure, Macedonia Baptist Church continued to worship at the Michigan Street location until March 31, 1974, when Macedonia made its grand entrance into 237 E. North Street. Reverend E.J. Echols and congregation of the First Shiloh Baptist Church were the guests. Sadly, on May 6, 1977, Reverend T.J. Merriweather retired after 13 years of service and on May 6, 1989, the church mourned his death.

In October, 1977, Reverend William Stoudemier was called as pastor and he served faithfully for two years. On May 4, 1980, Reverend Larry A. Boyd was called as pastor and he was installed the third Sunday of June 1980. While Pastor Boyd served as pastor, Macedonia held its mortgage burning service for 237 East North Street on January 23, 1983. Pastor Boyd served the church until September 6, 1991.

Reverend Herman Alston, Jr. was called as pastor of the Macedonia Baptist Church on June 1, 1992, and he was installed on July 12, 1992, by Reverend James L. Cherry Sr., pastor of the Aenon Baptist Church in Rochester, NY. Macedonia Baptist Church has weathered the storms of life through ninety years. The grace of God has sustained us, the goodness of God has reformed us and the mercy of God has maintained us. We are deeply appreciative of the former and late pastors, deacons, trustees, and members who helped to weather the storm, which has brought us to where we are today. With the help of our Pastor, Reverend Herman Alston, Jr., we will continue to grow in the service of the Lord. To God be the Glory!

Michigan Street Baptist Church
511 Michigan Street
Buffalo, New York

The congregation that became known as the Michigan Street Baptist Church was formally organized between 1832 and 1837. A historical sketch of the church written around 1908 by the Reverend Dr. J. Edward Nash, the church's pastor, states that "During the ministry of Elisha Tucker, Pastor of the Washington Street Baptist Church, a council was called to organize a colored Baptist Church, to be constituted of members from the Washington Street Church." (The Buffalo city directory for 1836 lists "Tucker, Elisha, pastor of Baptist church.")

The Washington Street Baptist Church was the first Baptist church to be established in Buffalo. It was apparently a white

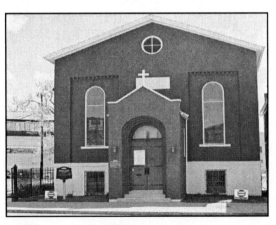

congregation that allowed blacks to worship in the facility. Reverend Nash's historical sketch further stated that during the fall of the year 1836, thirteen men and women withdrew from the parent church, and formed the Second Baptist Church of Buffalo. It is interesting to note that the first child sent out from the Mother Washington Church, was the Michigan Street Church. This faithful band commenced their worship in a small wooden building, over an undertaker's establishment at the corner of Niagara and Eagle Streets. A colored gentleman named William Munroe, had been ordained and was chosen as their minister, occupying all the positions that the name would indicate, Preacher, Pastor, Teacher, Janitor and Friend, his salary was raised by public subscription--after administering to this little flock for two or three years left them...

During the 1840s and 1850s, the Michigan Street congregation was served by numerous pastors including the Reverends William Monroe, A. Brown, Stephen Dutton, John Sharp, David Miller, Samuel H. Davis, D.W. Anderson, and J.S. Martin. Several of the church's early ministers were white. The white ministers included, "Mr. Verrinder, white, but not regular ordained," and "Reverend Mr. Jeffrey, a white ordained minister."

The campaign to build a new church began in earnest in 1842. The Reverend Mr. Sharpe, seeing the needs of worshiping in a better building, commenced to solicit funds to build a suitable house of worship, where this little flock might serve GOD according to the dictates of their conscience. In looking about for a site, Deacon Wm. Qualls and Peyton Harris, reported to the church a very fine piece of land on Michigan Street near Batavia, and after being duly delegated to purchase what site they thought best, they bought the land where the Church is now situated, Batavia Street being changed to Broadway. Reverend Sharpe went to England in search of aid, but was not successful and returned home. It was at this point that the women of the Church came to the front and united themselves into a Ladies Aid Society-object to aid the brethren in the building of a church....

One of the Ladies' fund raising projects was to sell needlework to the public. The fundraising continued and by 1844 the church had a membership of 56. In that year, "Mr. Peyton Harris succeeded in obtaining all of the lumber, brick and stone for the erection of the building and the Pastor, Reverend Davis, a mason by traded did the mason's work."

The church cornerstone was laid in 1845 and the congregation held the first services in the new structure in 1846. That was a memorable day, the first Sabbath in June 1845, when the Colored Baptist Church laid their corner stone. Work progressed rapidly on the building and the following spring they were able to worship in the basement. Mr. Sharp at this point left and the Reverend Mr. Jeffries, a colored preacher from Geneva took up the work; however his stay as a pastor was very short and in less than six months he departed for other fields, the membership being 66.

Samuel Davis and Mr. Miller were the next ministers, both of whom were ordained in the basement of the church. In 1848 the membership increased to 81 and the Sabbath school was organized.

By 1849 the church "announced that they had completed and dedicated their House of Worship. The building being worth $3500.00, and the land $2000.00." By 1851, church membership reached its highest point up to that date--93. "During all of this time the members were wondering how they would be able to raise enough money to finish their main auditorium.

After much prayer and consultation, the members decided to pay $10.00 annually for the rent of a pew."

Over the years the Michigan Street Baptist Church has been a central part of the history and culture of Buffalo's African American community. Even in the early decades of its existence as an independent institution, the theology of the African American church was not dramatically different from that of white Protestant churches of the ante-bellum period.

However, drawing from the mainstream Protestant revival doctrines, the independent black church articulated themes that addressed the unique needs and conditions of free people of color who felt a strong kinship to the slave community.

The African American church emphasized a theology of hope and optimism at a time when northern blacks were a small minority in an often hostile environment. The 19th century black population of Buffalo never reached more than 1.5% of the total Buffalo population. The pre-Civil War black church was the institution that was under the total control of blacks themselves. It was the institution that enabled African Americans to harness the energy and resources of the black community and to transform their ideas and aspirations into functional programs and activities. Like most Protestant religious institutions that advocated revival and reform doctrines, the African American church was active in the campaign against slavery. In addition, the African American church voiced strong opposition to racial prejudice and discrimination.

In 1842, the Michigan Street Baptist Church adopted a resolution opposing slavery. Black abolitionists like Frederick Douglass, William Wells Brown, Henry Highland Garnet, Martin Delany and others, made frequent stops in Buffalo to speak at anti-slavery gatherings. In fact, Brown was a resident of Buffalo during the 1830s. Although providing assistance to fugitive slaves was a violation of federal law, it was widely held that the Michigan Street Baptist Church was a station on the "underground railroad." By the late 19th century, such stories had attained legendary status. Members of the Michigan Street Baptist Church participated as delegates to the National Convention of Colored Citizens. Even in the pre-Civil War period the Michigan Street Baptist Church was considered the pride of Buffalo's African American community.

It had been built especially for an African American congregation. It was not a hand-me-down building. A newspaper clipping from the early 20th century stated that "old church records tell of the pride the congregation had in its first gas lights," which were installed in the mid-1850s.
At the end of the 19th century, there were still only three African American churches in the city of Buffalo. Because of its location and its involvement in the community, the Michigan

Street Baptist Church continued to be central to the life and history of Buffalo's African American community. The National Registry nomination form highlights two developments from that period: At the turn of the century two compelling community figures became associated with the Michigan Street Baptist Church and contributed greatly to the politicization of Buffalo's Blacks.

The first was the Reverend Dr.J. Edward Nash (1868-1957) who became pastor of the church in the 1890s and remained there for 61 years during which time he was instrumental in founding the Buffalo Urban League and the local branch of the N.A.A.C.P. In 1953 Potter Street behind the church was renamed Nash Street in his honor, and the National Conference of Christians and Jews presented him its annual Brotherhood Award in the field of human relations.

The second prominent figure associated with the Michigan Street Baptist Church was Mary B. Talbert, a neighbor and an active parishioner. [Mrs. Talbert earned a national reputation as a reform activist]. Her house was at 521 Michigan Avenue, two doors from the church (now demolished). In 1905 W.E.B. Dubois and other prominent African American leaders met at Mrs. Talbert's home (521 Michigan Avenue) and adopted the resolutions that led to the founding of the Niagara Movement. By 1930 the African American population of Buffalo had grown to more than 13,000.

"Gradually the Negro community grew up here taking possession of homes vacated by a line of owners and renters before them. They are among the oldest buildings in the city, less than four blocks from the business district and flanked on another side by a warehouse and light manufacturing area." As the northern black communities increased in size, the number of churches and other agencies serving those communities also increased. In time, other churches and community agencies began to assume some of the functions that the Michigan Street Baptist Church had performed for more than a century.

Although the Michigan Street Church has given up center stage in community life, its significance in the 19th and early 20th century history of Buffalo's African American community should be celebrated and memorialized by all future generations.

The Michigan Street Baptist Church at 511 Michigan Street was placed on the National Register of Historic Places in 1974. The Michigan Street Preservation Corporation is working to restore and preserve the site as a community landmark.

www.themichiganstreetbaptistchurch.org

Mt. Olive Baptist Church
701 East Delavan Avenue
Buffalo, New York

I n 1923, the Mt. Olive Baptist Church was organized under the leadership of the late Reverend James Hamilton inside the gates of Semet Solvay Company Plant. In 1924, the under the leadership of Reverend Clinton N. Polite, the church was moved outside of the Company gates, at which time Pastor Polite was called to pastor Tremont Temple Baptist Church in Buffalo, New York and later became Pastor of Calvary Baptist Church, Buffalo, New York. Reverend Merritt was called to fill the vacancy left by Reverend Polite. Reverend Merritt died in the early 1930's and Reverend James B. Benton became the next Pastor.

In 1941, Semet Solvay closed its village where some of the parishioners resided and Mt. Olive moved to 571 Clinton Street in Buffalo, New York and held its first service on the 1st Sunday in May, 1941 with approximately five families, to wit: Benton, Collins, Hatchett, Pitts and Robinson. The Church remained at this location for six months before purchasing and moving to 616 Clinton Street, Buffalo, New York. In November 1941, the Church was incorporated. On December 4, 1966, Mt. Olive moved to 629 East Delavan Avenue, Buffalo, New York where Reverend Benton served until January 1981.

In June 1981, Pastor William Gillison was called to pastor Mt.

Olive. Under Pastor Gillison's leadership our church has grown spiritually, financially and numerically. Since 1981, through our Pastor's guidance and being led by the Holy Spirit, the following ministries were organized and brought to fruition: the New Membership Class/ Ministry, Mt. Olive Inspirational Mass Choir, Male Chorus, Marketing Ministry, Theatre Workshop, Take Time To Care, Audio/Video Ministry, Prison Ministry and the Mt. Olive Development Corp., a not-for-profit faith based corporation.

In 1983, Mt. Olive Baptist Church along with Pastor L. T. Boyce and his congregation, celebrated the mortgage burning of 629 East Delavan Avenue, Buffalo, New York, two and one half years ahead of schedule.

In 1984, a vision from the Lord was given to Pastor William Gillison to build a new edifice to the Glory of God. How this would be accomplished only God would know. However, through much prayer and seeking God, the vision began to unfold. With his natural eyes he saw the existing conditions, limitations and constraints. He saw approximately 100 members in one Sunday morning service, in a half-empty building with no funds and no land. However, through God's eyes, He allowed Pastor Gillison to see abundance and possibilities. God showed him the land he would build on; a very large sanctuary filled with people-using kingdom principles, then He gave him a plan to acquire funds.

In the words of Solomon (II Chronicles 2:1), he began to share the vision and his heart "Behold, I will build a house to the name of the Lord my God, to dedicate it to Him." Making full use of Christ's teaching in Mark 11:23-24, Pastor Gillison and the faithful members of the congregation said for almost ten years, "It is time to build."

In February 1988, Mt. Olive Baptist Church purchased three and one half acres of land located at 701 East Delavan Avenue, Buffalo, New York and in August 1988, the Church held its Dedication and Worship Service on the land. In 1992, an additional one and one half acres of land was purchased giving the Church a total of five acres of land.

With continued faithfulness, prayers and contributions, the work was ready to begin. In December 1993, the site work began (clearing of the land, excavation, grading and pouring the foundation, etc.). In April 1984, building construction began.

Remaining faithful to the cause, Mt. Olive Baptist Church completed construction on its new Edifice in October 1995. To commemorate and celebrate the completion of its new Church, Mt. Olive held its first Black Tie Affair at the Hyatt Regency Hotel, Buffalo, New York.

On October 28, 1995, one glorious Saturday morning, the Mt. Olive Baptist Church congregation marched from 629 East Delavan to 701 East Delavan, Buffalo, New York into their beautiful Edifice; and on October 29, 1995 we held our first Sunday worship service. Presently, Mt. Olive holds two services on Sunday at 8:00 a.m. and 11:00 a.m. Since moving to our new location, we have been blessed with the following:

- Lawn Care Ministry
- Girl Scouts/Boy Scouts
- Young Men's Fellowship
- Scholarship Ministry
- Hospitality Ministry
- Mt. Olive Sanctuary Choir
- The Gospel Rhythm Show
- Purchase of 702 E. Delavan Avenue, Buffalo, New York
- Purchase of 917-921 E. Delavan Avenue, Buffalo, New York
- Expansion of Mt. Olive Development Corporation.
- *[FBS] Family-Faith Based Services is a home-based program, which provides services to at-risk families and is funded by the William B. Hoyt Children and Family Memorial Trust Fund and administered by the New York State Office of Children and Family Services.

*The Growth Opportunity Learning & Development Program [GOLD] is a federally funded quality after-school program designated for school-aged children grades Kindergarten through 8th; offering academic tutoring, computer classes, arts & crafts, recreation, mentoring and many other activities for youth.

In our future we will be doing more in Missions, both Home and Foreign. We will continue to build on our present Outreach Ministries to the least and the lost. Our efforts will intensify in helping our children prepare for a better quality of life.

At the same time we will be restoring and improving this House of God. Presently, we are looking at plans to build a Family Life Center and create an atrium in the front while looking for more land to possess.

Deuteronomy 1:8 "Behold, I have set the land before you: go in and possess the land which the LORD swear unto your fathers, Abraham, Isaac and Jacob, to give unto them and to their seed after them."

TO GOD BE THE GLORY!

Submitted by Mt. Olive Baptist Church

Mount Olive Missionary Baptist Church
72 Wasson Avenue
Lackawanna, New York

In 1938, a group of disenchanted members of the Ebenezer Baptist Church agreed to meet the third Sunday in September in a house at 16 ½ Melody Street, Lackawanna, New York to discuss their religious future. After considerable prayerful deliberation, they decided to form a church body.

Services continued to be held at this location until May 1, 1939 when this congregation moved to 97 Gates Avenue. We were organized into a church structure by Reverend McDavis. Our first pastor was Reverend Thompson. Some of the charter mem-

bers we recall were Mom and Pop Washington; Sister Alice Washington; Sister Eliza Anderson; Sister Charlotte Rivers; Sister Ora Mills; Sister Julia Williams; Sister Gussie Carter; Sister Emma Wright; Brother Beverly Woodson; Brother James Williams; Brother Henry West; Brother William Long; Sister Clara Salter; Brother Eddie Walker; Reverend Thompson and Reverend McDavis.

Church services were held at this location for a year, during which time the late Reverend Samuel B. Sutton served as our pastor. Under Pastor Sutton, the membership grew and the church began to prosper. In 1941, we purchased a building at 29 Fox Street and moved into it. After serving as Pastor for seven years, Reverend Sutton tendered his resignation in December 1947.

Reverend Tilmon C. Watson was called, delivering his first sermon as Pastor on January 5, 1949. Under his leadership the church experienced tremendous growth, existing auxiliaries expanded and new auxiliaries were formed. Pastor Watson led us in the construction of the edifice at 72 Wasson. During Pastor Watson's administration, the parsonage at 86 Wasson was erected and modified.

Many answered the call into the ministry under his leadership. Reverend Elijah Perry; Reverend Henry Mathias; Reverend Charles Page; Reverend Jesse Myers; Reverend Robert James; Reverend Anthony Benson; Reverend Nediume Westbrook; Reverend Luke Battle; Reverend Virgil Humphrey; Reverend Aaron B. Issac; Reverend Tony Birdsong; Reverend Harvey Fleming; Reverend Albert Ware; Reverend Kid Westbrook; Reverend Carris Johnson. Reverend Marshal M. Anderson served as Assistant Pastor. Those that are still pastoring today are Reverend Matthew Bushelon; Reverend Glen Raybon; Reverend Eddie Ware; and Reverend Lionell Clements.

Pastor Watson shared a vision he had of a new church structure and urged us to get serious about a building fund. After pastoring Mt. Olive for 25 years, Reverend T.C. Watson was called home to rest with God. Unity, Fellowship, holding to God's unchanging hand, and most of all, PRAYER kept this church family together.

From July 7, 1974 until May 28, 1978, Reverend Henry Wagner served as Pastor of this congregation. With his resignation, Reverend Eddie Ware served as interim Pastor, letting us know that without God we could do nothing. Giving us stability and to keep praying, for prayer is the answer, we sought God's guidance in selecting another leader.

The church called Reverend Brodie Johnson as Pastor on April 23, 1979. He preached his first sermon on May 6, 1979. He was a young energetic man that was prepared to meet the challenges of the church. Pastor Johnson set up the Building Fund, Membership Pledges, and a Scholarship fund.

Additional membership was added to the church. Also, two answered the call into the ministry. Reverend Keith Woodson and Reverend Pearson Miles are still pastoring today. We looked forward to many constructive changes in the days ahead of us. After serving two and a half years, Reverend Johnson resigned as Pastor on December 13, 1981.

Still praying and holding to God's unchanging hand, for God has never failed us yet, Reverend Ronald F. Thomas assumed the pastoral duties and was called as our Pastor on May 24, 1982 delivering his first sermon as Pastor on May 30, 1982..

Under Reverend Thomas' leadership, four young men were called into the ministry: Reverend Wendell Hamner; Reverend Darryl Thomas; Reverend John Elliott, and Reverend Larry Lewis, Sr.

Our membership continued to grow, and new fund raising techniques, the building fund, special projects and pledges. Under his direction we broke ground and began construction of our present edifice. By some miracle and undying faith in God, who is the head of all heads, gave us the strength to face the next battle. After pastoring for four years, Reverend Ronald Thomas resigned in June 1986. Reverend Wendell Hamner was then placed in change of the pulpit. Looking towards the hills from which cometh our help, the Lord once again had blessed the Mt. Olive family. On the fourth Sunday of August 1987, through Jesus Christ, we marched into our new edifice.

Reverend Robert L. Livingston was called as pastor December 1987. "Had it not been for the goodness and love of our Lord and Savior Jesus Christ, where would we be?" Reverend Robert Livingston pastored until July 2000. We pray that the Lord will continue to lead him.

On April 29, 2001, Reverend Dion J. Watkins was installed as Pastor of the Mt. Olive Missionary Baptist Church. God has sent us another God fearing man. On May 6, 2001, he delivered his first sermon as Pastor, entitled "When Jesus interrupts An Outcast." Luke 5:27-32. Reverend Watkins and spiritual leadership were what we needed to make our church family complete. He has been a blessing to each one of us here at Mt. Olive as well as the community. Reverend Watkins has taught us, loved each of us and dedicated his service both physically and spiritually. He has taught us that through our giving, God is putting us in a position to receive.

As we celebrate our church anniversaries, we look back to several accomplishments during Reverend Watkins' tenure. All have been done with the objective to continuing to advance the Gospel of Jesus Christ. During the leadership of Reverend Watkins, the membership has grown considerably; numerous members have united by Christian experience, baptism, and many members have rededicated themselves to the cause of Christ. Our youth membership has grown and they have become an integral part of the church.

Mount Olive has been blessed by God with a great heritage, a noble past, and a promising future that has the unlimited potential of untapped resources. What we will become will be determine by willingness to tell the world about "God's Amazing Grace" and our prayerful support of His Eternal Word. Prayer and hard work may mean the difference between life and eternal death.

This history of Mount Olive Missionary Baptist Church is extensive and arduous. To accurately display the history required many long hours. However, those hours capture a history that is rich in culture, reflects the preservation of tradition, and records the advancement of a congregation blessed by God. History is wonderful.

WITHOUT A PAST, WE HAVE NO FUTURE!

Mount Zion African Methodist Episcopal Church
1061 Sycamore Street
Buffalo, New York

In 1976 while attending Bethel African Methodist Episcopal Church, Reverend Hammett discussed with his dream of organizing a church with Bethel's pastor, Reverend G. Grant Crumply who thought it was a good idea. He stated that there was a need for another African Methodist Episcopal church in Buffalo. Reverend Hammett would name the church Mount Zion. He had united with Agape African Methodist Episcopal Church and shared his dream with Pastor Fred Lucas who encouraged Reverend Hammett to pursue his dream.

The organizers of Mount Zion are Reverend Milton Hammett, Fanny M. Hammett, Terry O. Hammett, Harvey T. Hammett, and Virgil Hammett. Five years later on Saturday, April 11, 1981, Mount Zion African Methodist Episcopal Church held its first worship service at 6:00 PM. In attendance were pastors, ministers, and members from other churches: Reverend Fred A. Lucas Junior, pastor of Agape African Methodist Episcopal Church along with Reverend Robert Locke, Samuel Pitts, Richard A. Stenhouse, Thomas Davis Jr., and Tony Pinn; Reverend Eugene McAshan, pastor of Bethel African Methodist Episcopal Buffalo; Reverend Henry Lewis, pastor of Delaine Waring; Reverend Clara R. Castro and associate Minister Pedro Castro;Reverend Samuel King, pastor of First Church Lockport; Reverend Carrie Collins, pastor of First Church, Olean.

Reverend Fred Lucas Jr. was the speaker and the text for his sermon was "Encouraged to Step out into the Deep" from Luke 5:1-6. With Reverend Lucas in the pulpit, the church launched its Mount Zion Project to the glory and honor of God.

The first Sunday morning worship service was held on April 12, 1981. Pastor Hammett's sermon came from Proverbs 16:6 – 9, and his focus was the seventh verse and his subject was "I am going to please God." Present were Reverend Robert Locke, an associate minister from Agape African Methodist Episcopal Church along with Shirley Davis on piano and Jackie Allen.

The church worshipped first at 357 Grider Street and later on Bailey Avenue. Shortly thereafter the current location at 1061 Sycamore Street was purchased.

In 1994, Reverend and Mrs. Hammett returned to their home in South Carolina. Their son Reverend Virgil Hammett was appointed to take the helm of Mount Zion and he served until

early 1995. When Reverend Anne Hargrave Pinn was appointed pastor of Mount Zion, Sister Aileen Lewis asked for and was given permission by her pastor, Reverend Wayne Johnson Sr. to accompany Reverend Pinn to Mount Zion. Ms. Lewis stayed at Mount Zion for three years and helped to organize the Lay Committee, the usher board. The generosity of members and friends was a blessing to Mount Zion. Dr. Anthony Pinn donated the cross, candlesticks and vases in memory of his grandparents, Mr. and Mrs. Ashley S. Hargrave Sr. Friends of Mount Zion donated monies to purchase a communion table.

In 1996, the Fannie Mae Hammett Missionary Society presented Sisters Sharing, and many of God's people helped to make this a meaningful experience. In 1998, Mount Zion stepped out in faith and began the Kidspace program. It was our attempt to provide a safe place for children to common received the help they needed. The program ran successfully for approximately five years.

In October 2003, Mount Zion paid off its mortgage. Presiding Elder Ernestine Ward came to Buffalo to burn the mortgage and to celebrate this accomplishment. On June 13, 2005, Reverend Anne Hargrave Pinn lost her fourteen year battle with leukemia, and in July, Reverend Herman Boyer Jr. as appointed to serve as pastor to the Mount Zion congregation. He came with a spring in his step, a smile on his face, and determination to preach the word in season and out of season. His motto: "There are no big I's or little you's in the body of Christ." Mount Zion, the little church that could.

From *Taking the Old Path and Preserving Our Legacy*, compiled by Florence Hargrave Curtis, Western New York African Methodist Episcopal Conference District 1, Historiographer

Mt. Zion Missionary Baptist Church
1334 Calumet Avenue
Niagara Falls, New York

Mount Zion Spreads Her Wings and Rejoices

Mt. Zion was born in September 1962 when a faithful group of committed Christians organized a series of prayer meetings and services on the lawn of Deacon James L. and Ada L. Williams at 2813 Thirteenth Street. When the weather became inclement, they met in the heated garage of Mr. Eugene and Mrs. Ruby Cook at 3605 Highland Avenue.

These founders prayed together and played together. It was not unusual to see them playing croquet on one of their lawns. These interactions engendered respect and camaraderie that facilitated their ability to establish a viable religious institution. They had a vision and they were committed to principles of Agape. They perceived themselves as missionaries and understood fully that the church's responsibility had to be extended into the community. Education was an important vehicle through which they hoped to accomplish this; therefore they created special programs for youth.

This group immediately created a structure that would permit them to carry out their mission of worshipping and converting others to their faith. James L. Williams, general chairman, presided at the organizational meeting and other officers selected were Queenie Parchue, secretary, and Deacon Henry Thomas, treasurer. The Board of Deacons and Trustees conducted the spiritual and administrative functions of the church. Edison Tucker presided over the original Board of Deacons with J.D. Williams, Sr., James Ellis, T.R. Davis, Willie Hall, Theodore Kimble, W.P. May, John H. Smith, Henry Thomas and James L. Williams. The Board of Trustees was responsible for fiscal matters and the church's security. Eugene Cook was founding chair with Grady Cook, Virble Humphrey, Aubrey J. Smith, Roosevelt Tabb and Wilbur T. Haynes, who also served as secretary.

The church operated through several auxiliaries. Theodis Kimble was Sunday School Superintendent and Deaconess Ruby Cook headed the Board of Christian Education. Ethel Smith was president of the Deaconess Board. Minerva Cook headed the adult choir and Robert L. Jenkins, Jr. was president of the youth choir, while Alpha Jessie headed the Usher Board and Foy Flournoy headed missionary societies that originally included the Ruth and Naomi Circles.

The church was called Mt. Zion Missionary Baptist Church to symbolize its elevation of the principles and teachings of Christ and that set it apart from the secular world, yet cemented it to that world.

James L. Williams, Henry Thomas and Juanita Humphrey signed the incorporation papers on September 23, 1962 and they were recorded in Niagara County on September 27. Soon the church purchased a small church structure at 1332 Calumet Avenue.

On July 14, 1963, it called the Reverend W.R. Vaughn, Dean of Theology at the historically black Bishop College in Texas, to be its founding pastor. Reverend Vaughn was installed in October, 1963 and served until November 1968 when he accepted a position in Detroit. His administration focused upon strengthening the church and increasing its membership. Reverend Vaughn and Mrs. Viola Vaughn, a teacher in the public schools, worked diligently with the auxiliaries to establish a viable education program for the youth. In addition to the Sunday school program, there were BYPU and Vacation Bible School and recreational programs for children. Reverend Vaughn was cognizant of the fact that the church's mission extended beyond its walls and that it was incumbent upon it to address social ills that the community faced. One of these was housing. Niagara Falls had an old stock of substandard housing and African Americans tended to be segregated in the poorest areas. Several established churches felt the need to do something about the housing and established the Interfaith Housing Authority.

Mt. Zion was the first African American church to join this body and Reverend Vaughn appointed Lillian S. Williams delegate to the organization. The Interfaith Housing Authority's work ultimately led to the construction of the Unity Park Housing development, an integrated housing facility.

After a series of guest ministers the church hired Reverend Matthew J. Bushelon who assumed his position on the second Sunday in March, 1970. Immediately, Pastor Bushelon proposed to build a new edifice to accommodate the growing church membership. A building committee was established to explore the possibility of purchasing land. Their findings indicated that the costs for property exceeded the church's budget for the project. Reverend Bushelon encouraged the church body and urged them to be patient. In February 1971, Moore Business Forms, Incorporated presented the church with the deed for the land which is now the site of Mt. Zion. The Land Dedication service theme "A Time to Build Up" taken from *Ecclesiastes* was held on October 10, 1971, and the church initiated a building fund drive with a goal of $30,000 which they reached in nine months. Services began in the new building on August 4, 1974.

During Reverend Bushelon's administration, the ministerial staff grew and several young ministers John Owens, Rocelius Jessie, Victor Griffin, Arthur Todd, and Anthony Polk worked with Reverend Bushelon. The black Baptist Church has been reticent to address gender issues and is notorious for restricting women's roles in the church.

However, Reverend Bushelon appointed Valerie Haynes, the first female assistant minister, an indication that he understood that progressive churches embrace the important contributions that women clerics have made to the profession. Women also began to serve on the Trustee Board and Ocile Jessie, Paulette Shine, and Stephanie Williams Cowart and Joyce M. Williams were members; both served as church treasurer. The only remaining bastion of male prerogative is the Board of Deacons.

During the Bushelon administration, the Board of Deacons expanded to include Roosevelt Tabb, Bennie Watson, Wilbur T. Haynes, Sr., Nathaniel Robertson, Earl Billups, Leon Smith, and George Williams. A younger generation of men including Charles A. Walker III, Hilary Hillary, John Haynes, Theodore Haynes and Kenneth Laurel joined also.

Mt. Zion became renowned for its music. The Male Choir, the Joyettes Gospel Singers, The McCray Family Singers and the Adult/Young Adult Choir brought many souls to church and many joined. Today the gifted Diana Reeves, an ordained minister, is Mt. Zion's Minister of Music.

Church auxiliaries increased as its vision expanded. The Nurses Guild, under the leadership of Jacqueline Walker Lynch, spearheaded the Health Ministry. It offered blood pressure clinics, and sponsored the annual Mother and Daughter banquet. The James L. Williams Memorial Scholarship Committee, established in 1985 by the children of Deacon Williams, institutionalized the church's ability to support the educational goals of its youths.

When Reverend Bushelon died on February 12, 2007, Mt. Zion was well respected in the community. It played an important leadership role in Baptist Associations and it was poised to embark upon other growth areas in the community. After Reverend Bushelon's death church associate pastors conducted services and a search committee was established to hire a permanent minister. Prospective candidates also conducted Sunday services, Sunday School and Prayer Meetings.

Reverend Ronald Jennings contributed to the youth ministry and the Young Adult Spiritual Growth Ministry was organized with Larry Henderson, Rashad Williams, and Allen Q. Cowart providing the leadership, respectively. The church appointed Reverend James Missick interim pastor and he served in this capacity for three months. During his tenure he also was interested in expanding the youth ministry. Ikeyah and Company, a liturgical dance team, was established with Mrs. Missick as advisor and choreographer.

In October 2009, Mt. Zion appointed the Reverend Timothy J. Brown as its third pastor and ushered in "The New Beginning." Reverend Brown brings his infectious smile, energy and enthusiasm to Mt. Zion. He also brings his vision for expanding the church membership through its young people. Dozens of people have joined during the Brown administration; and he also established a radio ministry on WUFO radio in Buffalo, New York that has been a successful vehicle for outreach. Reverend Brown further has energized the youth by bringing more of them into Bible classes and re-organizing the youth choir. Over the past year, the Health Ministry has been expanded.

In 2010, special exercise programs including Pilates and group walking sessions have been offered and for the first time in 2011 the church partic-ipated in the  National HIV Screening Program. Reverend Brown initiated a new administrative structure. In 2011, Deaconesses, who largely served in supportive roles, assumed the duties and responsibilities required of Deacons, but retained the title of Deaconess. Under Pastor Brown's leadership, we look forward to more new beginnings.

"Mount Zion rejoices today in the joy of her salvation. She stretches forth her mighty arms that all who will may enter and be blessed....Beautiful is her situation, the joy of the whole earth is Mount Zion."

Lillian S. Williams,Ph.D. Church Historian and Archivist

Muhammad's Mosque 23
5 Walden Avenue
Buffalo, New York

Student Minister Brother Dahweed Muhammad said, "We want make people aware of the direct contact that Minister Malcolm X had with the pioneers, in setting up Muhammad Mosque #23 in Buffalo, ". "Minister Malcolm traveled to the area several times to visit the family of Ora-Lee X Lewis (McQuiller). We know her now as Ora Lee Khalid Lewis-Delgado. Her brother, Bobby McQuiller brought the teaching of the Most Honorable Elijah Muhammad to Lackawanna, New York in 1953.

According to Brother Dahveed, Sister Ora-Lee also received letters and phone correspondence directly from the Most Honorable Elijah Muhammad, who sent Minister Mal- colm to the area, in response to a great many letters that Elijah Muhammad was receiving people   in Buffalo and Lackawanna, because of the work and effort of Brother Bobby McQuiller. The family of Levi and Kathrine X. Hawkins, with daughters Maryann, LuCinda, and Carol, began attending study with Bobby McQuiller in Lackawanna in 1954.

Eventually, Minister Malcolm moved the study group to Buffalo to Sister Ora-Lee's house at 78 Brunswick Blvd., chronicled Brother Dahweed. "From there it was moved to the house of Levi and Kathrine X. Hawkins at 44 Butler Avenue. Minister Malcolm eventually sent Minister Thomas J. X and his assistant Minister Robert J. X from Hartford, Connecticut in 1956 to continue growing the Buffalo study group. Minister Malcolm visited the homes at 78 Brunswick Boulevard and 44 Butler Avenue several more times in

support of the growing study group. The group eventually achieved the status of a Mosque and received its number 23 in 1957, under the leadership of Minister Robert J. W Williams.
There are copies of original letters of guidance and instruction written by Minister Malcolm to the ministers that he installed here.   Minister   Malcolm   typed   the   letters,   and   wrote handwritten notes in the margins.
Brother Dahveed provided the following timetable of significant events and individuals of those early days.

- The study group begins meeting at Brother Sandy and Sister Catherine's home on Wyoming Street in Buffalo, NY.   In 1982, the Muhammad Study Group moves the meetings to Harambee Books and Crafts on Main and Utica.
- Minister Abdul Halim Muhammad is appointed minister in 1985.
- The study group moves the meetings to a storefront on E. Ferry and Cornwall Avenue and moves to E. Ferry and Goodyear thereafter.
- Muhammad Mosque #23 moves to 5 Walden Avenue in 1990.[14]

---

[14] "A Tribute to the Pioneers: A History of the Nation of Islam in Buffalo" *Buffalo Challenger* February 19, 2011

New Cedar Grove Life Changing Church
100 Old Maryvale Road
Cheektowaga, New York

The New Cedar Grove Life Changing Church, formerly Cedar Grove Missionary Baptist Church, was founded by the late Reverend M.J. Lynch in March, 1955 at 133 Bennett Street (home of Sister Frances Powell). The membership consisted of only five (5) members. On April 1, 1955 the church moved to 500 William Street. After worshipping there for a short while, on July 20, 1956 the church moved to 123 Sycamore Street at Pine Street. Then the church relocated to the Glenwood Hall, 292 Glenwood Avenue for a larger place of worship. In September 1959, we moved to 108 Clinton Street and worshipped there for fifteen (15) years. On August 18, 1974, the Lord blessed us to move into 878  Humboldt Parkway. Each time we relocated was a result of membership growth. We have had four wonderful pastors to lead the flock thus far: the Founder, Reverend M.J. Lynch, Reverend James Loynes, Reverend T.L. Ransom and our present Pastor, Reverend Melvin Brooks.

Great progress was made under the leadership of Reverend T. L. Ransom. Some of Buffalo's greatest musicians were brought in under Reverend Ransom's pastoral leadership. He served our church for over thirty years. Following Reverend Ransom's retirement, in February of 2000, we were blessed with a leader and mighty man of God, Pastor Melvin Brooks. He has brought us nothing short of the Word of God. Through his leadership many hearts and lives have been changed.

Because of such noticeable changes in lives, we've added to our present church name. We are now known as "New Cedar Grove Life Changing Church" (Baptist).

Several ministries have been added to the church: Seniors, Singles, Evangelistic, New Members, Youth, Children's Church, Men, Women, Culinary Art, Media, and Greeters.

Because of the importance stressed by Pastor Brooks to do ministry, renaming our service was necessary. The following are now changed: Benevolent to "Helps and Needs"and Sick Committee to "Visitation of Love." God has truly enriched our strives in kingdom building. Inasmuch as we had given our current building, where we worship a brand new look, God put it on our Pastor's heart to strive for excellence.

Our new edifice located at 100 Old Maryvale Road on a 5.5-acre property and highly visible from the Kensington Expressway is the former Mother of Divine Grace Church. We can now increase our depth of ministry which will include additional administrative office space and an educational component.

Blessed are we here at the New Cedar Grove Life Changing Church! May God forever bless and keep us.

www.newcedargrove.com

New Covenant United Church of Christ
459 Clinton Street
Buffalo, New York

New Covenant United Church of Christ was founded on September 20, 1974 with the merging of two churches, the former Lloyd's Memorial Congregational Church (which was joined with the newly formed United Church of Christ in 1958) and St. Peter's United Church of Christ. Salem United Church of Christ became part of the congregation in 1976. Members of the Concordia Bethany United Church of Christ joined the congregation in 1988. Each of these churches had a long and distinguished history of dedicated Christian service in the Buffalo community.

Along with St. Peter's, Lloyd Memorial United Church of Christ, incorporated in 1914, is a cofounder of New Covenant which had its origins in a group which split from Bethel AME church because of a concern for moral reforms. In 1964, Lloyd constructed a building at Spring and Clinton Streets, and New Covenant worshipped there until its move to 459 Clinton Street. New Covenant began under the dual pastorate of Reverend Jimmie L. Sawyer until 1975 and Reverend Philip Smith until 1978.

Reverend Will J. Brown was called to serve as an interim pastor in 1979. A few months later, he was called as part-time pastor, a position he held for nine years. In 1988, he accepted the call as the fulltime pastor of New Covenant. Under Pastor Brown's leadership, the membership was spiritually uplifted through Bible class, Sunday school, worship service and the celebration of various liturgical events. Congregants have been added to the membership, each participating in new membership classes where they learn the history of the United Church of Christ and its Christian foundation.

Blessings have been overflowing. An addition was added to the church consisting of secretarial and trustee offices, and two lavatories. Pews, carpet, a sound system, and a television were installed, two vans purchased and updates were made to the fellowship hall, kitchen and the pastor's office.

New Covenant has sponsored a weekly food pantry for the surrounding community, and through our gifts and offerings New Covenant supports missionary activities around the world and locally. We participate in the New York State Conference and the Western association of the United Church of Christ. Pastor Will J. Brown served for thirty years at New

Covenant United Church of Christ in Buffalo. He retired as Senior Pastor November 14, 2010, becoming senior pastor emeritus. Reverend Will J. Brown transitioned from his earthly home to live eternally with the Lord on July 13, 2011. The associate pastor, Jacquelyn Ross Brown, assumed the senior pastorate December 1, 2010. Standing on the mountain of accomplishments in our past, we clearly embrace our mission of ensuring that the gospel is preached and sacraments are celebrated as well as ensuring the provision for peace, justice and liberty to all that we meet.

Submitted by New Covenant United Church of Christ

New Hope Baptist Church
543 Richmond Avenue
Buffalo, New York

The New Hope Baptist Church was organized on July 15, 1925, by Mrs. Henrietta Bennett, Mrs. Ethel Bowers, Mrs. Isabella Long, Mr. John Long, Mrs. Esther Mae Murphy, and Mr. Robert A. Spencer. The first meeting was held in Bristol Hall, located on Bristol Street near Jefferson Avenue. At that time, there were fifteen members. The Lord blessed the congregation to grow and by

September 1925, church services moved to Central Hall on William and Jefferson Streets. Reverend R. Reed was designated to organize the church officers and to preside over business matters. Having no appointed pastor, various ministers officiated each Sunday.

In November 1925, Reverend L.A. Holloway was called to the pastorate. On September 26, 1926, while he served as pastor, New Hope Baptist Church was incorporated. Reverend Holloway resigned in 1927 and ministers of the church conducted services until another pastor could be called. Reverend Burgess, Reverend Slearin, and Reverend McGarrah complied with the church's request.

In late September 1928, Reverend Nathanial Andrew Mason was called to pastor. Still on the move, the church had moved to an aged church building on old Vine Alley. A house and a parcel of land were purchased on Union Street and plans for a church building began. Reverend Mason, along with the church members, participated in the construction by actually laying many of the bricks that became part of the church foundation and exterior. Upon completion, the cornerstone of the first official church home for the New Hope Baptist Church was laid at 63 Union Street in 1932. Praise God!

The final mortgage on this property was burned on June 18, 1944. In the late 1950's, due to urban reconstruction, New Hope was faced with the challenge of relocating.

In November 1960, led by Reverend Mason, the congregation marched into its new home at 543 Richmond Avenue. In September 1962, after 34 years of dedicated, consecrated service, Reverend N. A. Mason, New Hope's pioneer pastor, was called from labor to reward.

The Reverend Joseph William Moore accepted New Hope's call to the pulpit on May 6, 1963. He labored with New Hope for thirteen years, and departed this life on February 1, 1976.

From February 1976 until July 1977, New Hope Baptist Church was without a shepherd. Associate ministers, Reverend Samuel Byrd and Reverend Walter Peacock, along with "Sons of the Church", Reverend J.B. Williamson and Reverend Charles Jennings, ministered to the needs of the church. Pastors from sister churches throughout the city willingly graced the pulpit in a spirit of love and concern for the New Hope family. On July 25, 1977, the church extended a call to Reverend Lee Roy Jefferson. After serving for nearly three years, Reverend Jefferson resigned on May 5, 1980.

The Reverend Paul Frederick Thompson was called to the pastor New Hope on November 2, 1980. He served the congregation for twenty years. When Reverend Thompson retired, he was given the title "Pastor Emeritus." In October 2002, Reverend Herschel Chapman, Jr. was called to pastor the New Hope Baptist Church.

New Life World Harvest Restoration Center
416 Louisiana Street
Buffalo, New York

In 1995, the late Dolores Adams was the original member and initiator of the Commodore Perry Full Gospel Church.

Dolores Adams lived in the Perry Projects and saw that there was no local church in the area. She spoke to her niece Veronica Baker and asked if she would ask her Pastor if Bethesda Full Gospel Church would start a bible study for the residents of the Commodore Perry Projects. Veronica spoke with Pastor Badger regarding this request and was asked to get together with Pastor Keith Scott who was the head of the Evangelistic Department.

Shortly thereafter a small bible study began in Dolores Adams home once a week. Dolores Adams spoke with management of the Commodore Perry Projects to see if they would allow Bethesda to use the community center to have church services. The purpose of the church was to provide religious services, ministry and hope to the residents in the area which was considered by many to be one of the most dangerous areas in Buffalo, infested with crime, drugs and poverty. Pastor Keith's passion was to see change in this community which led him to reach many people, to convince them that God had not given up on them. Pastor Keith Scott went home to be with the Lord in March 2008.

On April 27, 2008, Melvin and Pamela Taylor were sent out by Senior Pastor, Bishop Michael Badger to serve as intern Pastor to comfort the remaining members and to continue the ministry in the community. There were four members remaining when they started.

Every Saturday afternoon in the month of August they held a community cookout serving hotdogs, hamburgers, chips and drinks. By the end of September, there were 40 people attending services, most of them were youth.

A Sunday School Service for youth was started, a mid-week Prayer and Bible Study for adults and our first Membership Class was held in November 2008. In January 2009, we started a Boy's Scout Troop, a ministry for young girls, monthly discipleship classes, a monthly men's breakfast to men 13 years of age and older, and a weekly radio broadcast "New Life."

The church is seeking to purchase a facility in the area to serve as our future worship center, in the mean time we are preparing to add another Sunday service by the end of the summer at our present site in the Commodore Perry Auditorium. On April 26, 2009 Melvin L. Taylor Jr. was installed as the Pastor. The name of the church was changed to New Life World Harvest Restoration Center, "a place of fellowship and love."

www.newliferestorationcenter.org

Pentecostal Temple Church of God in Christ
618 Jefferson Avenue
Buffalo, New York

Pentecostal Temple is a charter member of the Churches of God in Christ, headquartered in Memphis, Tennessee. The church has been a standard bearer of holiness with a Pentecostal message with apostolic order and Episcopal structure. Bishop Charles Henry McCoy, the founder of the Pentecostal Temple Church, has proved to be a progressive visionary, administrator, prophet, priest and leader of the church in Western New York.

The church had humble beginnings in 1924, when it was started by the late Elder Emmett Lowther. Elder John L. Lewis succeeded him and named the church Zion Church of God in Christ on August 31, 1948. Elder McCoy, who succeeded Reverend Lewis, renamed the church Pentecostal Temple on September 15, 1958.

In 1962, Pentecostal Temple moved from 512 Jefferson Avenue to its present location at 618-620 Jefferson Avenue. The Temple location was a trucking garage that was renovated into a stately sanctuary by Elder Charles McCoy and eight members of the church. The "faithful few" diligently followed their present day visionary. Many days and months of hard work produced a church that would eventually host jurisdictional meetings for years. lder McCoy and the members of the church were proud that the Lord had blessed them with the skill to renovate what appeared to be a useless facility into a sound structure that would house HIS glory for decades to come. In 1968, Elder McCoy was consecrated to the office of Jurisdictional Bishop of Western New York Second. This great honor was accompanied by his conferral of a Doctor of Divinity degree from Trinity Hall College and Seminary in 1971.

An astute spiritual leader and devout saint of God, Bishop McCoy continued to dream for the saints of his local church and the people of the fifty-five churches within his jurisdiction.

In 1977, Bishop McCoy began to desire a building or structure large enough to host the jurisdictional conventions and serve the community through various ministries of the church. When premier downtown land became available (a city square block), Bishop McCoy and others worked with the late Alice Hill to secure the downtown block of Clinton, Adam, Eagle and Watson Streets. Presently, the C. H. McCoy Convention Center has completed Phase I of the development. Bishop McCoy worked tirelessly to assure "the saints would have a place to worship the Lord."

Elder Matthew L. Brown began his tenure as pastor of Pentecostal Temple C.O.G.I.C. in 1996. Since then church has grown from fifty active members to over three hundred members under the dynamic leadership of Elder Brown, Pastor-Teacher. He has been successful in establishing the ministry as a beacon of hope to countless individuals and families served by the organization. He aggressively challenges the notion that church exists simply for the proliferation of the local assembly, but rather views the church as the change agent; pointing the way to purpose, peace and prosperity for the community it serves. A consummate educator, Elder Brown has successfully established the Pentecostal Temple Bible Institute (PTBI), an extension of Logos Christian College and Graduate Schools in Jacksonville, Florida. Brown also serves as the Superintendent of the Trinity District, in the Second Ecclesiastical Jurisdiction of the Church of God in Christ, Western New York. Our church's international ministry includes partnership and support of three ministries in Montego Bay, Jamaica.

The church currently is working with six faith based businesses and sourcing contracts and real estate for the massive development proposed on the eastside of Buffalo, New York, while providing mortgage opportunities for home ownership to its members.

The Temple is reflective of urban contemporary ministry positioning itself for the end time harvest. Television, radio, print and internet venues are utilized to reach fallen and lost humanity.

Pentecostal Temple today continues the economic strategy of our beloved Pastor and Bishop by initiating our Temple Community Development Corporation, Temple Federal Credit Union (application), In His Face Productions (audio & video production), Temple Resource Center and Pentecostal Temple Bible Institute.

www.pentecostaltemplechurch.com

Promiseland Missionary Baptist Church
227 High Street
Buffalo, New York

P romiseland Missionary Baptist Church had its beginnings in a house on Caldwell Street in Memphis, Tennessee. The cornerstone was laid by Reverend Davis in 1910. In 1920, Reverend Twillus Davis was called to Buffalo to conduct a revival in which 95 converts were added to the church. The group then worshipped in a store front on the corner of Pratt and Clinton Streets and it was known as Friendship Baptist Church. After becoming the pastor of the church, he moved to Hickory and Clinton Streets. In October 1939 Reverend Davis organized the Promiseland Missionary Baptist Church at the corner of Vary and Jefferson. The church was incorporated in 1942 and moved to its present location at the corner of Mulberry and High Streets in 1955.

Under the leadership of Reverend Davis, several ministries were established such as, the Sunday school, Youth Choir, Junior Usher Board, Religious Education for Buffalo School Students, Missionary Society, Faithful Chorus, Senior Choir, Young Adult Choir, Senior Usher Board and Pastor's Aide Society. In 1977, Reverend Davis invited long time friend Reverend Sidney O.B. Johnson's son, Minister Horace (Billy) Johnson to assist at Promiseland. Reverend Davis served as pastor until his death in October 1979 at the age of 99.

Minister Johnson was asked to serve as interim pastor until a Pastor was elected. He served in this capacity for two years. While in the process of obtaining a new pastor, Reverend Charles Jennings was invited. He was then elected as Pastor and was officially installed on July 28, 1981. Under his leadership, the church moved forward establishing ministries such as the Male Chorus, Young Adult Department, Social Committee and reinstated the Nurses Guild.

After 25 years of service, Pastor Jennings retired in December 2006 and relocated to South Carolina. Pastor Gregory Deas was then elected as Interim Pastor after Pastor Jennings' retirement. After six months of faithful service he was then elected and installed as Pastor on April 25, 2008.

Under the leadership of Pastor Deas, the church has grown in attendance and finance, with new ministries being established and reinstated: the Youth and Adult Choir, Praise Team, Praise Dancers, Family and Friends Day, Vacation Bible School, Friday Night Evangelistic Service (Friday Night Fights), Men of Standard (Men's Group). Also, six deacons were ordained and eight associate ministers, with numerous baptisms and many reclaimed member- ships. The  church is on Facebook and has its own website. Pastor Deas is a man of God who preaches and teaches what thus saith the Lord under the anointing of God. Lives are being changed and delivered. It is his desire that Promiseland Missionary Baptist Church be a place of refuge for every individual looking for help for the soul. One of Pastor Deas's favorite sayings is "Almost Saved Is Totally Lost!"

To God be the Glory for the things that He has done.

Redeeming Fire Fellowship Church
145 Lewis Street
Buffalo, New York

I t was 10:24 am as I stood still on that stage in complete shock. In that grand ballroom, camera flashes made it hard to see, the band's intense playing made it difficult to hear, while the 200 in attendance charged the stage. I had just given the benediction to the first service of the Redeeming Fire Fellowship Church, with approximately 190 individuals received as its congregation.

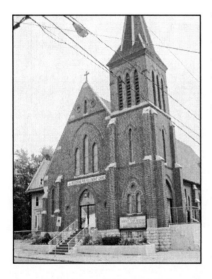

The Lord had brightly shown His glory in the Adam's Mark Hotel that Sunday morning on April 19, 2009, but He wasn't through. We were a church without a home. But Ephesians 3:20 says, "He is able to do exceeding abundantly above all that we ask or think, according to the power that worketh in us. "After days of driving around Buffalo looking at vacant Rite Aid and Family Dollar stores as possible sites for our church, Elder Vincent Benton and I drove to meet a realtor about the vacant property of the Precious Blood Roman Catholic Church. As I drove up to the property I immediately knew this was the Lord. But one problem-the property was already under contract. The following Sunday morning I stood before the Redeeming Fire congregation telling them that I believed we had found our home. I passed out directions to the property, and asked everyone to meet there following the worship service. After loading up all the sound equipment from the ballroom, I was among the last to leave the hotel. When I arrived at the property, it was the most beautiful sight to see.

People (out of virtually every house) were standing in their yards, all looking toward the church at the crowd of people, chaotically parked in the street, as they walked around the church. We voted that this was the home of the Redeeming Fire Fellowship Church, joined hands and sang "We Shall Overcome," and claimed it all in prayer. Prayer does change things. In the morning, I received a call from realtor that the contract on the property had fallen through.

After some negotiation, eighteen days after our first worship service, I was seated inside a law firm five stories above downtown Buffalo, signing the contract for the cash purchase of the former PBC, Rectory, and Administrative building, located on the east side of Buffalo at 140-5 Lewis Street .

Within weeks the congregation was organized into groups and we diligently went about the work of cleaning up the property, while contractors went about the work of renovation. On June 8, 2009, we held our first worship service in our house! Members and friends from across the city came to share in this glorious event: God favored us as He has done nearly each worship service with new members added to our family. Redeeming Fire Fellowship Church has quickly become a church seriously committed to the work of the gospel of Jesus Christ. Among the normative ministries at work in local churches, we have initiated Project FIRE (Faith Initiative to Revolutionize the Economy) to target over 74,000 Buffalo residents that are forced to live in poverty by providing donated clothing and canned foods to help alleviate the struggle to provide for the family, and allow for the reallocation of funds.

Redeeming Fire Fellowship Church is not another rising church. It is a community of faith, highly favored by the Most High Lord for our righteousness, in His Son Jesus the Christ. Today we are a family of over 400, and we sincerely love another in Christ. We worship Christ. We witness his favor. We win over the enemy.   http://therffc.org

Second Chance Ministries
381 E. Ferry Street
Buffalo, New York

On January 5, 1999, Reverend Arthur H. Boyd, the founder and President of GROUP Ministries Inc., shared his God given vision with two friends, Prudence Fuller and Kenny Smith. He had already told his wife, Michelle Boyd that he felt a need to minister to the community on another level. After much prayer and fasting, Reverend Boyd received a vision from our Lord and Savior, Jesus Christ to build a house of worship. For six months, meetings were held at the Boyd home to study a plan to organize this worship center. The work moved to GROUP Ministries to accommo date the

people interested in joining this mission. As plans developed, Arthur and Michelle experienced three separate occasions in which the words 'second chance' stood out profoundly.

The first time Reverend Boyd preached at E.C.M.C., a gentleman said to him, "You have given me a second chance." The second time Reverend Boyd was reading a book Michelle had given him entitled, *Fresh Wind, Fresh Fire*, in the last chapter, on the last page, the last paragraph, the last sentence, was the statement, "All the people want is a second chance." The third time occurred at Calvary Baptist Church during morning prayer. A female prophet while speaking to the congregation spoke a prophetic word to Arthur and Michelle saying God is giving you a second chance. She repeated it three times. The confirmation was clear and the Worship Center was named, SECOND CHANCE MINISTRIES: A Community Church. The foundation for this ministry was based on Acts 2:42: "They continued steadfastly in the apostles' doctrine," at the end of the chapter Luke writes," and the Lord added to the church daily such as should be saved."

The text also provides us with the five strong principles to give us Purpose, to build the Kingdom and follow God's agenda; Vision, to build a house of worship; Mission- creating a community of believers who love God, love themselves, and love God's people. The five principles are worship, fellowship, discipleship, ministry and evangelism, which put us in balance with the will of God, being a purpose driven church.

On December 31, 1999, Reverend Boyd held the first worship service at 1490 Jefferson Avenue, with the blessing of his home church, Elim Christian Fellowship where T. Anthony Brunner was the Senior Pastor. That day 56 people took membership in Second Chance Ministries.

On January 23, 2000, Reverend Arthur H. Boyd was officially conferred to the position of Arthur H. Boyd Pastor/Teacher of Second Chance Ministries. The host site was our mother church Elim Christian Fellowship. Officiating was Pastor T. Anthony Brunner in a ceremony enhanced by the ordination of our Deacons, Wilbert Davis, Louis Keye, Frank Black, Arnold Romer, William Gault, and Ronald Sessum.

On April 28, 2002, by the grace of God, Arthur H. Boyd Pastor/Teacher and his congregation moved to the new worship center at 381 E. Ferry Street purchased in pledges of close to $30,000 and seed money from our mother church, Elim Christian Fellowship. Second Chance Ministry is celebrating eleven years in ministry and continues in covenant partnership with the Turning the World Upside Down Ministry under the leadership of Bishop T. Anthony Brunner.

Currently, Second Chance Ministries has 310 members on the roll. The Ministerial Staff consists of Pastor Arthur H. Boyd, Senior Servant, Avon White-Pastor of administration, Darieck Foster-Pastor of Prison Ministry, Kenneth Simmons- Youth Pastor, Minister Thomas Lewis, Minister LaMertis McKnight, Minister Deadra Smith and Minister Forrestal Gray. Chairman of Trustees-Jeannie Lewis, Chair of Deacons- Deacon Rodney Menifee, Executive Secretary-Monica Jeffries, Church Clerk-Glynis Lackey Ministry Leaders Culinary-Astor Davenport, Children's Church-Deacon Jonathan White, Christian Education-Ava White , Community Health-Mother Louise Lindsey, Hostess Ministry- Cynthia Glen, Intercessory prayer – Minister LaMertis McKnight, Men's Ministry-Pastor Arthur H. Boyd.

Also Missing Link- Kenny and Deadra Smith, Music Ministry-Sister Drea' , Mothers Ministry-Mother Betty DeVaughn, Prison Ministry-Pastor Darieck Foster, Transportation- Deacon Kevin Lett, Ushers Ministry-Joyce Peach, Women's Ministry-Michelle Boyd, Youth Ministry- Pastor Kenny Simmons. First Ministerial Staff: Reverend Arthur H. Boyd, Minister Darieck Foster. Original Trustee Board: Kenneth Smith, William Gault, Glenda Green, Beverly Lipkins, Thelma Killabrew. Original Acting Deacons: Ronald Sessum, Arnold Romer, Rick Smith. First acting secretary: Prudence Fuller. First acting clerk: Ava (Kemp) White.

Charter Members are Mother Elease Boyd, Frank and Brenda Black, Rosetta (Brunner) Menifee, Yusekica Clark , Ida Cooper, Candace Daniels, Wilbur Davis, Darieck Foster, Prudence Fuller, William (Cris) Gault, Thomas and Glenda Green, Ava (Kemp) White, Louis and Joan Keye, Thelma Killabrew, Beverly Lipkins, Arnold Romer, Kenneth and Deadra Smith, Leslie Stewart, Rickey Smith, Ronald Sessum , Avon White.

To God be the Glory!

Submitted by Second Chance Ministries

St. John African Methodist Episcopal Church
917 Garden Avenue
Niagara Falls, New York

The First Black Church in Niagara Falls, New York

Early in 1906, a small number of African Methodist Episcopal members began holding services in a home on Eleventh Street. Later that year, Reverend Joseph Styles, Presiding Elder of the Manhattan District came to Niagara Falls at the request of the members and organized the St. John African Methodist Episcopal Church. Reverend A. L. Wilson was appointed the pastor. The congregation moved to 306 Niagara Street, but continued to search for a more appropriate site. The members located property at 477 Main Street and incorporated as St. John African Methodist Episcopal Church. It is recognized as the first black church in Niagara Falls, New York.

Reverend Joseph Gomes and Reverend L.B. Langford served as the next two pastors of the church. Reverend J. Leo Pottinger was appointed on May 27, 1923. During his tenure, land was purchased at 155 13th St. in the presence of Joe Plato, Royal Palmer, James Steward, John Malloy and Frederick Ford. The cornerstone was laid on November 9, 1924. For the first time, the congregation had a permanent place to worship.

The new church consisted of a first floor sanctuary which seated 120 people, a basement which housed a small kitchen, a dining area and a boiler room. An apartment on the second floor served as a parsonage. At this time, Reverend D. B. Barton was the pastor. Under his leadership a $100 Club was organized to raise funds to pay off the mortgage of the church. Two years after the $100 Club's inception, a special service was held to celebrate a successful campaign which raised $4900, enough to retire the church's debt.

The succeeding pastors served as follows: Reverend Henry L. Gault, Reverend T.H. Tyson, Reverend Norman Brown, Reverend H.L. Gumbs, Reverend A.A. Amos, and Reverend G.C. Hall. On September 28, 1951, Reverend Edgar L. Huff was appointed pastor of St. John. He and his wife, Anna and their daughter, Doris saw the church experience epic growth. The 120 seats could no longer accommodate the congregation, so Reverend Huff launched the Venture of Faith program. He led a relocation and building program by inaugurating a fundraising drive. Four lots bounded by Center Avenue, Ninth Street and Garden Avenue were acquired. On March 15, 1961, the groundbreaking was held for the new church and the cornerstone was laid by Electric Lodge 49 P.HA. The new St. John African Methodist Episcopal Church was formally dedicated on May 26, 1962, by the Right Reverend George W. Barber.

The site of the new church is historically significant because the house that sat there was a stop on the Underground Railroad. There was a cave beneath the house where passengers on the railroad were hidden until they crossed over to Canada and freedom. A monument now stands on this site commemorating it as a place where slaves stopped to rest, find succor and food on their journey.

The new building which houses the St. John congregation consists of a sanctuary with a large choir loft, a fellowship hall with the commercial styled kitchen, a dining area, restrooms, three storage areas a library and a ministerial office, a communications room to class/storage areas, and the federal credit union's office and storage area.

Reverend Huff made Niagara Falls and the community at large his home. He served as a member of the city of Niagara Falls urban renewal agency and president of the NAACP; the Highland Avenue Bridge was named in his memory and the fellowship hall at the Niagara Community Center and Girls Club Association was renamed in his memory as well. When Reverend Huff died in 1980, he had served St. John African Methodist Episcopal Church for 29 years.

Reverend Carlton Woodward succeeded Reverend Huff. A new parsonage was purchased at 1228 Calumet Avenue in 1981, and the sanctuary was renovated when a basement was added to the church.

The youth and young adult choir recorded an album on June 9, 1984 under the musical direction of Reverend Robert Lowe and Brother Roger Walker Junior. Vanessa Bell Armstrong was the featured artist and the anniversary was dedicated to the memory of Benita Water, a past president and faithful choir member.

Reverend Fred Tennie succeeded Reverend Woodward. Reverend Joseph Robinson Sr. was appointed the next pastor. The Reverend Huff Bridge was rededicated and the church's fellowship hall was rededicated in honor of Reverend Huff as well. Reverend Trevon Gross was appointed as the next pastor. Reverend Gross assisted in the raising of funds for the building of a high tech community center to provide tutoring and computer training, job placement, union organization, and self-esteem seminars for single black women.

Reverend Micah Chandler, the next pastor, held a "We Remember Momma" program to honor the church's mothers in May 2000. The first family and friends homecoming celebration was held at Whirlpool Park on August 27, 2000. Reverend Jocelyn K. Hart became St. John's first female pastor. A charismatic preacher, she loved children's programs and vigorously supported them. Each second Sunday, she relinquished the pulpit to the youth of the church. Her tenure ended when she was transferred to Philadelphia in February 2006. Reverend Stanley Gordon Smith came to Niagara Falls from Pennsylvania. He was appointed to the pastorate in February 2006 while working to complete his master of divinity degree, so he was required to commute from New York to Pennsylvania until his graduation in May 2006. One of his immediate goals was to have St. John choirs to reclaim their past level of function. In November 2006, St. John African Methodist Episcopal Church celebrated 100 years of service to God and the community.[15]

"Reverend Beulah Leslie James is the second woman pastor in the history of St. John's. A Harlem-born grandmother of three who has preached everywhere from St. Croix to South Africa, she comes from a family of preaching women. She was the first female president of the Niagara Ministerial Council, a group of pastors and other clergy in the city. At St. John there were some 300 members, including an inspired choir. Pastor James almost doubled Bible Study participation, and she also started the church's monthly newsletter, the St. John Journal. "[16]

Reverend Robert L. Reynolds is the current pastor.

We have come this far by Faith.

---

[15] *Taking the Old Path and Preserving Our Legacy*, compiled by Florence Hargrave Curtis, Western New York Conference African Methodist Episcopal Church, Historiographer

[16] Daughter of a preaching family makes history" *Buffalo News*, January 24, 2010

St. John Baptist Church
184 Goodell Street
Buffalo, New York

In 1927, Reverend McCarley was led by the Holy Spirit to organize the St. John Baptist Church with four members: Alice and Mabel McCarley and Joseph and Dora Kelly. One year later with a membership still under ten, he considered giving up his church, but in a vision he was taken to a large church and shown a huge congregation over which he would pastor. Accepting this as an inspiration of the Holy Spirit, he continued laboring to bring souls unto the Lord. For many years, in addition to his pastoral duties, Reverend McCarley tended the coal furnace, shoveled the snow, and opened and closed the church for services. During much of that time he didn't receive a salary, but he enjoyed fellowshipping with his members 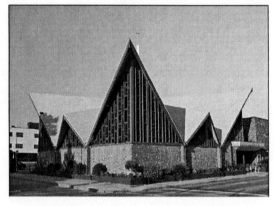 who often prepared Sunday dinner for him and his family.

After occupying storefronts at 657 William Street, 481 and 616 Clinton Streets, St. John was incorporated in 1930, and soon after moved to 92 Monroe Street (Little St. John). The small congregation had room to grow and in the ensuing years the Lord showered His blessings on the church. The Brown, Martin, Aiken, and McCarley families were a part of the swelling congregation that also hailed from South Carolina. Pastor McCarley preached; souls were saved, and the members and choir praised God in song on Sunday mornings and at afternoon and evening services.

By the mid 1940's, a larger house of worship was needed and the German Evangelical Church at 183 Sycamore Street was purchased for $21,000, and the members marveled at the blessing of this three storied edifice. Marching from 'Little St. John' on October 5, 1945, members rejoiced as they entered the spacious sanctuary with a balcony and pipe organ.

Pastor McCarley and his family also moved from the rear apartment at 92 Monroe to the upstairs apartment at the new church at 183 Sycamore Street. The congregation had a mind to work and the mortgage was paid off in less than two years. Sunday mornings, the processional song for the choirs followed devotion with Mrs. Lillian Beckham playing celestial notes on the pipe organ. Afternoon and evening programs featured the songs of the Brown Brothers and the Bell Aires; St. John had a glorious ministry in music.

The Senior Choir, the Gospel Chorus, the Bells, the Youth and Young Adult Choir, the Junior Choir, and the United Voices became vehicles for a collective spiritual experience not only for St. John but also for the community of Western New York.

Nearly two decades later in the aging Sycamore Street building, Sunday school classes spilled over into the balcony, the sanctuary, and the basement. During worship services, the ushers sat chairs in the aisles to seat the parishioners. This overcrowding led to the formation of the Building Committee to explore the possibility of expansion. After several options were explored, the decision to build a new church was made and the architect, Wallace V. Moll was selected to design it. Reverend McCarley stated, "This building will outlive me and those generations to come." The site selected for the new edifice included properties at Maple, Michigan and Goodell Streets. After it was cleared, the groundbreaking was held. Members of the Building Committee, Charles Locke, Julius Day, Ben Washington, Andrew Brown and others, were given tasks to monitor the rising structure.

Early in 1966, the newly constructed edifice was reaching completion of the sanctuary and a balcony, a single story educational wing, a lower level with a kitchen, and large meeting area.

On May 1, 1966, prayers of thanksgiving and joyful exuberance erupted. Led by Ben Washington, the parade marshal, the processional began at 183 Sycamore and ended at 184 Goodell Street where the marchers, the media, family members, friends, Fruit Belt residents, and expectant onlookers waited patiently to enter the new edifice.

After the official ribbon cutting ceremony, the speeches and the prayers, the officers, members, and visitors assembled in the sanctuary, the ushers took their stations, the choirs filled their seats in the choir stand, and Reverend Burnie C. McCarley stood humbly in the pulpit looking at a huge congregation. For six years, Reverend McCarley served the congregation in this edifice until he was called from labor to reward on March 10, 1972. He had served as pastor for four and a half decades.

In 1971, the annual revival was slated to begin at the St. John Baptist Church in Buffalo, New York. When Reverend Otis Moss Sr. who had been scheduled to preach became ill, his friend, Reverend Bennett W. Smith Sr. was sent to replace him. The following year, Reverend Smith was invited to return to preach during a Sunday worship service at St. John. Following the death and sixty day mourning period of our founding pastor, Reverend Burnie C. McCarley, the congregation and the Board of Deacons agreed to extend an invitation to Reverend Smith to become the second pastor to lead the St. John congregation On the fourth Sunday of June 1972, Reverend Smith preached his first sermon as pastor from the subject, "Invitation to Discipleship."

Reverend Smith forwarded both an ambitious spiritual and secular agenda. However, shortly after his arrival, he recognized that some of the parishioners contested the connection he had developed between religion and politics. In spite of this, Reverend Smith continued to challenge the congregation and the disenfranchisement of the African American community. As a result, new members were asked to complete the voter registration form as a part of their St. John church membership application. He was the Buffalo coordinator of Operation PUSH. Some of the many accomplishments throughout Reverend Smith's tenure include changing the infrastructure of the church, identifying women to fill key positions, significantly increasing the body of believers, and providing Christian education for African-American children.

His *Watch Them Dogs* sermon garnered a Grammy nomination and currently has videos on *YouTube*. In addition, he served for four years as president of the 2.5 million member Progressive National Baptist Convention, which held its annual convention in Buffalo in 1997. He oversaw the construction of the four million dollar, three story Reverend Dr. Bennett W. Smith Sr. Family Life Center designed to serve the surrounding community. On August 7, 2001, Pastor Smith went from labor to reward. He had served the St. John family for nearly thirty years and God had used his voice and words to shape lives and develop faith in "a more excellent way."

The third pastor in the history of the congregation, Minister Michael Chapman is the second generation of the Chapman family at St. John.

Called to the ministry and licensed in 1988 and ordained under the Reverend Dr. Bennett W. Smith, Sr., Pastor Chapman served for over a decade as the youth minister and assistant to Pastor Smith. Minister Chapman benefitted from the sermons and teachings of Reverend McCarley and the mentoring and instruction of Reverend Smith. Tent revivals on Buffalo's east side became part of Pastor Chapman's evangelistic effort to fight violence with faith: "We just believe the word of God will have an effect on the community." His style of ministry invited a more relaxed dress for Sunday worship as well as basketball games with the youth.

St. John Baptist Hospice Buffalo House was opened in June 2008, and it was Pastor Chapman`s flagship initiative to improve end of life care and end of life transitional needs in the minority community. The development and construction of this faith based community hospice facility is the first of its kind in the United States. St. John is a church with only three pastors in its over eight decade history: each with a distinct call to ministry; each serving in challenging eras, each addressing the needs of the community; all serve God's people and seek to do His will. The St. John Campus provides the spiritual and secular community access to the ministries of the church, housing for families and the elderly, education and recreation for many, and finally end of life care.

Amos and Beavers Collection 2011

St. Martin De Porres Roman Catholic Church
555 Northampton Street
Buffalo, New York

On August 22, 1992 four parishes, St. Matthew, Our Lady of Lourdes, St. Benedict the Moor, and St. Boniface, took a bold move of petitioning the bishop of Buffalo to merge these parishes and erect a new one. After almost two years of prayer, reflection, study, and painful discussion, the parishes came to the conclusion that in order to find a renewed and stronger faith community, they must first lose their individual parish identities. Leaving their homes of worship, these four congregations joined together on a pilgrimage of faith officially beginning the new parish of St. Martin de Porres on March 7, 1993.

Joining their resources together, new life was breathed into this new church community that found its temporary home within a Catholic high school auditorium and later for a few years in yet another formerly closed church sanctuary. Musically, choir members came together from each of the communities to form the Mass Gospel Choir of St. Martin de Porres still under  the direction of their founding director, Mrs. Ella Robinson.

For many Christian communities, the task of building a new church building especially in this day and age is a dream. Working hard to secure at least one half of the monies necessary, our faith community accepted the challenge and Bishop Henry Mansell consecrated our new church home at 555 Northampton Street on March 11, 2000; it was the first new Roman Catholic Church built in the city of Buffalo in fifty years.

We still look forward with a sense of excitement and some trepidation. We still dream of being debt free, building a state-of-the-art Parish Center that would host a history of the rich heritage of the properties and an African American Catholic Gospel Music Resource and Recording Center.

Inspired by the missionary zeal and example of St. Martin de Porres, abiding by Christ's call to serve and nourish the spiritual needs of all people, we the people of God, led by the spirit, in the Catholic Diocese of Buffalo New York, united by faith and committed to the continuation of an evangelizing mission, unconditionally invite and welcome all to share in our oneness in Christ. Prompted by the workings of the spirit and empowered by baptism, St. Martin de Porres Church seeks to call forth the people of God to utilize their gifts in order to strengthen our Christian community, to evangelize, to preach, to teach, to serve and to reconcile.

St. Martin de Porres stands as a living testament to our heritage. We call one another to conversion of heart in order to transform unjust structures and to hear the cry of the poor.

Submitted by St. Martin de Porres

St. Paul's A.M.E. Zion Church
610 East Eagle Street
Buffalo, New York

In June of 1925, a small group of believers left St. Luke's A.M.E. Zion Church (then located at 174 East Eagle Street) to start a new church. Earlier in the year a decision was made by then Rt. Reverend. William L. Lee, Reverend. Henry Durham (pastor of St. Luke's), and others, voted to expand Zion in Buffalo. The new church – and the second designated Zion -- assembled in Bristol Hall, 278 Jefferson Avenue, on July 29, 1925 under the name St. Paul's Mission African Methodist Episcopal Zion Church.

The first church purchased was a building located at the corner of Emslie and Oneida Streets. The congregation met there for seven years, then moved to a "store front" located at the corner of Howard and Watson Streets. During the typical cold Buffalo winters, church members supplied coal to heat the large, one-room facility. In June 1936, Reverend. Noah H. Bexley was appointed pastor of St. Paul's. During his tenure, the Western New York Conference (Bishop C. C. Alleyne presiding), consisting of Reverend. Stephen Gill Spottswood (later a bishop), Presiding Elder William Frances, Reverend Derrick M. Byrd, and others purchased the 623 East Eagle Street church from the Evangelical German Church. The congregation moved to that location in October 1936, the word "Mission" was dropped from the church's name, and it became St. Paul's African Methodist Episcopal Zion Church.

On a cold December evening in 1983, after the choir walked across the street from the "old" church to the newly built 610 East Eagle Street edifice to test the acoustics in the new sanctuary, there was a loud explosion.

A worker dropped 550-lb. propane tank that began leaking, found an accelerant, and exploded. Five firefighters and two civilians were killed instantly and scores of others were injured.

The stained glass windows of the new edifice were shattered, but no church members were injured. The following year, the congregation entered the fully restored church, which was fully paid for during Reverend. G. Michael Tydus' 17-year pastorate.

St. Paul's A.M.E. Zion Church celebrated its 85th anniversary in 2010 and we look forward to another 100 years in His service, and in service to the community. Pastors – 1925-2010

John Wesley Jackson (founder) 1925-1934

Russell M. Brown 1934-1935

John A. Springfield 1935-1936 (local preacher, St. Luke's)

Noah Bexley 1936-1938 (Eagle St. property purchased)

Simon Peter Triggs 1938-1941

Harold M. Kirnon 1941-1945

William S. Sims, Assistant 1945

Gilbert H. Coffey 1945-1947

Emory C. Proctor 1947-1956

Leroy J. Montgomery 1956-1960

Joseph C. Curtis 1960-1961

Jacob C. Ruffin 1961-1975

Frederick Bryant 1975-1976
G. Michael Tydus 1975-1993 (church built and paid for)

James Christopher 1993

Vincent T. Frosh 1993-2000

James R. McMillian, Sr. 2000-2005

Robert E. Williams 2005-2006

Dr. Lawrence E. Lucas, II 2006-present

Submitted by St. Paul's African Methodist Episcopal Zion Church

St. Philip's Episcopal Church
15 Fernhill Avenue
Buffalo, New York

St. Phillip's Episcopal Church was founded May 30, 1861 and celebrated 100 years in May 2011; it is the seventh most senior African-American congregation in the United States. Today, we rejoice in the wealth of community that this parish continues to provide.

St. Philip's was founded in the basement of our former church at 45 Elm Street. The congregation selected and adopted the name St. Phillip's on July 9, 1861. From 1861 to 1865, St. Philip's was under the supervision of a white clergyman, Reverend Witherspoon, who conducted services and led the congregation until it was able to call a full-time Rector. The Reverend Samuel L. Berry of St. Luke's, New Haven, Connecticut, became  the first black full-time Rector of St. Philip's Church, an independent colored congregation in September 1865. St. Phillip's was incorporated in September 1866 and canonical consent was given by The Right Reverend Arthur Cleveland Coxe, the second Bishop of the Diocese of Western New York.

In 1865, Reverend Samuel Berry, along with the Reverend James T. Holley, founded the Protestant Episcopal Society for promoting the extension of the church among colored people. This society eventually became the Union of Black Episcopalians, an organization that fights to remove racism and encourage the growth of members with African roots in our church today. In July 1876, Reverend Joseph Robert Love became the Rector of St. Philips's. Philip's grew steadily and after the turn-of-the-century, it felt the need for expansion. In 1921, under the leadership of the Reverend Edmund Bennett (1916 – 1923) and the vestry, our congregation moved to 166 Goodell Street where we remained until 1974. As urban renewal projects developed in the neighborhood, the building on Goodell Street was scheduled to be demolished, and we were forced to relocate.

We moved to our present location at Sussex Street and Fernhill Avenue. The property currently consists of the church, its adjoining parish hall, the adjacent rectory and two adjacent vacant lots. The parish survived the parish hall fire in 1975, and in 1988 funded the restoration of its organ. St. Philip's from its inception has been and continues to be a predominately African-American congregation and it remains the only parish in the diocese of Western New York that can be so described. The congregation is a working-class and middle-class/professional and draws members from all over Buffalo and the immediate suburbs.

The story of St. Philip's is God working through its people. St. Philip's has been the church home of Buffalo's first African-American architect, John E. Brent who became the second African-American in history to design a YMCA for blacks, the Michigan Avenue YMCA; Mrs. Geneva B. Scruggs became the first woman elected to the vestry and was bestowed the Bishop's Cross; and Wilhelmina MacAlpin Godfrey a magnificent artist and humanitarian. We are proud of our heritage and tradition influenced significantly by the late Reverend Osmond H. Brown(1923 – 1956). This patriarch became the first black Canon in the Episcopal Church of the United States. We strive to maintain our tradition of "High Church" worship in this tradition as a means of expressing our love of Jesus and our parish.

Reverend Kenneth S. Curry succeeded Father Brown in 1957 and continued to provide leadership and guidance needed to take us through some very difficult years. Father Curry, for a period in his tenure, served as Dean of the 13 parishes in the Central Erie Deanery. During his rectorship, he started the St. Philip's Community Center with an afterschool program for neighborhood children, and it has been in continuous operation since its founding more than 40 years ago. The right Reverend E. Don Taylor, in 1973 was invited by The Right Reverend Carol B. Robinson, Bishop of Western New York, to become the Rector of St. Philip's. He served the parish for five years and during that time he started and developed the St. Philip's School of Music and Boys' Choir. His arrival at St. Philips in 1974 coincided with the move to our present location.

He worked long and hard to reorganize the parish and to his credit began a movement of new outreach programs. Included was the music school which operated for ten years. At its prime, the Boys' Choir toured Europe and placed fifth out of 16 at an international boys' choir competition in Vienna, Austria.
Father Taylor later became the Bishop of the Virgin Islands and presently serves as the assistant Bishop of New York City. The Reverend Walter Bryan (1979 -- 1981) was active in community organizations and was particularly effective in programs for youth and Christian education for adults. The Food Pantry, established under his tenure, is still maintained today.

Under the leadership of the Reverend James Manning (1982 -- 1987) the traditional "Sung Mass" flourished, vestments were restored, and new lay leadership was developed in the area of acolyte training and liturgical participation. The Reverend Julius D. Jackson (1989 -- 1995) remembered for his ministry to the sick and bereaved, trained and enhanced the role of lay Eucharistic ministers in the parish. During his tenure, African-American hymns became a regular part of weekly worship through the use of the hymnal Lift Every Voice and Sing II. The Reverend D. Antonio Martin (1998 -- 2001) worked to reorganize the ministries at St. Philip's to more effectively carry out the mission. During his tenure our great sign greeting the community was constructed and placed on the corner of Fernhill and Grider Avenues.

The Reverend Gloria Payne-Carter began her ministry at St. Philip's in June 2005. Her institution as the 11th Rector of the parish was held on September 17, 2005, and her tenure continues as the Rector today. St. Philip's is especially proud of her sons who were ordained to Episcopal priesthood and ministry: the Canon Laughton D. Thomas, James E.P. Woodruff, the Reverend James Oliver Lee, the Reverend James Williams, and the Right Reverend Michael B. Curry, Bishop of the Diocese of North Carolina. We claim and raise up the ministries of the Reverend Richard Meadows and the Reverend Andre Williamson as they do God's work in other denominations.

Submitted by St. Philip's Episcopal Church

Trinity Baptist Church
2930 Bailey Avenue
Buffalo, New York

I n 1916, Shiloh Baptist Church was formed at the home of Mattie Causey. Membership increased and a building was secured at Clinton and Hickory Streets. Membership continued to increase and the congregation rented a building at 34o Jefferson Avenue. The Shiloh Baptist Church split into two congregations. The original group took the name of First Shiloh Baptist Church and the second group used the name Shiloh Baptist Church.

By 1917, Shiloh Baptist Church had moved to a former fire house at 96 Spruce Street and officially became the Trinity Baptist Church. Until 1922, Trinity utilized "Supply Ministers" to carry out its worship services before electing its first Pastor, Reverend John Monroe.

The first wedding held at Trinity Baptist Church uniting John H. Hackney Sr. and Mary J. McCurry. From 1932-1934, Reverend N.B. Harris served as Pastor. Reverend J.B. Crooker served as Pastor from 1934-1936. Reverend Julius T. Sparks elected Pastor and the church continued to grow both spiritually and financially. In 1940, Pastor Sparks and the congregation purchased 41 Spruce Street for $13,000.00. The burning of mortgage and placement of the cornerstone occurred in 1944. In 1958, Reverend J.T. Sparks retired as Reverend Steven L. Hargrove who had served as assistant Pastor was elected Pastor. Extensive renovations were done and a centralized treasury was set up. The Cozetta Smith Scholarship Fund was also set up under his leadership.

Reverend J.T. Sparks passed in 1961. Reverend Hargrove served as Pastor for seventeen years, passing away in 1975 while still serving as Pastor. The church continued under the leadership of the Chairman of the Deacon Board, Deacon William V. Callahan Sr.

In 1977, Reverend Joseph Davis was elected Pastor leading the congregation to purchase a baby grand piano and the first church van. Reverend Davis began working immediately organizing and adding programs to make the church operate more efficiently. On Sunday, October 25, 1987, Reverend Davis announced his retirement. For the next two years the church was led by Deacon Jethro Hale, Chairman of the Deacon Board.

In 1989, Reverend David Lucas was elected interim pastor and becoming Pastor the following year. Rev Lucas resigned in 1992 accepting the call to pastor a congregation in Mt. Vernon, New York.. Reverend Albert J. Gupton Sr. elected Pastor after Trinity was led by the capable and spiritual hands of Deacon Jimmie Underwood, Chairman of the Deacon Board.

Reverend Gupton reinstituted the Nurses Guild and started a radio ministry. He led the remodeling project of our building which was constructed in the mid 1800's. Reverend Gupton mentored and encouraged one of Trinity's sons, Deacon Bennie D. Jemison Sr. and on September 29, 1998, licensed him to preach the word of the Lord and Savior Jesus Christ.

In 2002, after a sequence of meetings the congregation voted to purchase the Bethany Lutheran Church at 2930 Bailey Avenue at a cost of $105,000.00 cash. Our treasurer, Deacon John Hackney was instrumental in finding this jewel sent by God. Prior to the move into our new edifice, Reverend Albert J. Gupton Sr. resigned.

Deacon James Chandler Sr. Chairman of the Deacon Board, led the congregation in our first worship service in our new building on June 3rd. Reverend Joseph Davis returned to conduct the first Holy Communion service in our new sanctuary. Deacon Chandler continued to lead our congregation until January 9, 2005 when the Reverend Bennie D. Jemison Sr. was installed as Pastor of Trinity Baptist Church.

The Trinity Baptist Church Historical Museum opened on February 27, 2005, through the hard work of the Curator Bernice Wiggins, and Assistant Curator, the late Diana C. Perry. We have a rich history at Trinity Baptist Church, and we are blessed with five members that joined at 96 Spruce Street. In 2007, the Trinity Baptist Church celebrated our 90th church anniversary. Nine Decades, "Walking Worthy of the Lord."

The 2008 implementation of the Trinity Baptist Church 5 year mission: Through the Holy Spirit....by having faith and being holy, strengthening leaders, leadership and loyalty to Our Lord and Savior Jesus Christ.
We are continuing our five year mission: Finances, Family and Fellowship. We are in God's hands, realizing it's the Lord's doing, as we travel the upward way gaining new heights every day.

Submitted by Bernice Wiggins, Church Historian

True Bethel Baptist Church
907 East Ferry Street
472 Swan Street
Buffalo, NY

Eight members attended the first service of True Bethel Baptist Church on November 8, 1961, in the home of Mr. and Mrs. Elijah Tillman. They chose the name True Bethel which means "True House of God." On February 26, 1962, the late Reverend Peter Trammell, Pastor of Calvary Baptist Church ordained Reverend Floyd Summers as the new

Pastor of True Bethel Baptist Church located at 457 Genesee Street, Buffalo, New York. Pastor Summers served as pastor from 1961 to 1964. Reverend O.C. Amos served from 1964 until 1967. He was followed in 1967 by Reverend Columbus L. Perkins who served until 1969. Reverend C.B. Jones pastored the congregation for over twenty years from 1969 until 1992.

In 1993, True Bethel was in search of a pastor and Reverend Motley Spells gave Sister Essie Brock a card with the name of Darius G. Pridgen. After hearing him preach only three times, Albert Swain, chairman of the Deacon Board felt moved to accept Reverend Pridgen for a trial period of two years. After nine months, the church voted him into a full term as Pastor of True Bethel Baptist Church.

Under the leadership of Pastor Pridgen, the church has grown tremendously in the last fifteen years from a congregation of two dozen members to well over 4000. True Bethel moved from 491 East Ferry Street to the current location at 907 East Ferry Street, and in 2002, added its second location, in downtown Buffalo at 472 Swan Street and 1112 South Avenue in Niagara Falls, New York.

In the fall of 2004, Pastor Pridgen and the congregation were recognized nationally for the opening of the first Subway franchise on a church campus.

Pastor Pridgen says, "The sandwich shop is really just an extension of the church and provides opportunities for marketing the gospel of Jesus Christ."

While all of the church's locations have Sunday worship services, many of True Bethel's ministries engage the congregation in service: Drama, Evangelism, Hospitality, Music, Prayer, Security, Transportation and Ushers. True Bethel Charities is an arm of True Bethel Baptist Church which ministers through its Taste of Faith food pantry, True Bethel Clothes Closet and Nehemiah Arms, transitional housing, all of which seek to provide for the daily needs of the congregation and the wider community.

Pastor Pridgen's vision for True Bethel is to spread the gospel of Christ in such a way that adults, youth and even a child would understand the teachings of our Lord and be able to

 apply them to their lives continuing to follow God's direction. True Bethel is in the final stages of building a multi-duplex sanctuary for worship services of the congregation.

Pastor Pridgen often says, "If I can change the way they think, then have helped them." This ministry believes in the true commission of helping others and letting them know that their appearance is not what matters to God, but their heart is the center of his attention.

But the Lord said to Samuel, "Do not consider his appearance or his height, for I have rejected him. The Lord does not look at the same things man looks at, the outward appearance, but the Lord looks at the heart." *(1 Samuel 16:7)*

www.truebethel.org

Walls Memorial African Methodist Episcopal Zion Church
55 Glenwood Avenue
Buffalo, New York

The dream became reality, and the late Reverend Rudolph L. Wells was given permission to organize an African Methodist Episcopal Zion Church in the "Cold Spring" area. Selecting a place was the next step. The first place of worship was at the Seventh Day Adventist Church located at 130 Northland Avenue. Once the site was selected, on November 7, 1948, the Reverend Wells assembled a group of people. With the holding of Sunday School and Morning Worship, the then Trinity African

Methodist Episcopal Zion Church was formally established. This would be the first African American Methodist body in the Cold Spring area. Founding members were Mrs. Brunson, Sarah Johnson, and Minnette Wells.

This group worked with Pastor Wells to locate and purchase a site of their own to give them a sense of permanency. In 1954, the church contacted the late Bishop William Jacob Walls about their finding a building and the desire to purchase the same: 455 Glenwood Avenue.

At the Western New York Annual Conference in June 1955 the name of the church (Trinity AME Zion) was changed to the William Jacob Walls Memorial AME Zion Church in recognition of Bishop W. J. Walls' effort and support in establishing another AME Zion Church in Buffalo.

Walls Memorial had become the third AME Zion church in the city, but then the only one in the Cold Spring area. On October 27, 1955, the congregation moved into its new location at 455 Glenwood Avenue.

At the 1955 Annual Conference, the Reverend Wells was transferred to St. Mark AME Zion Church in Lackawanna, New York.

The list of pastors after him reads as such:
> The Reverend C. J. Henderson (1955)
> The Reverend Melvin Peter Linder (1956?-1958)

Under The Reverend James T. Hemphill (1958-1972) this ministry the church grew. Due to his vision, the first Head Start Program in America was started. The church's ministry opened its doors to countless young people whose lives were blessed and this work is fondly remembered even today by those touched by it. Under his leadership, on October 16, 1966 the mortgage on the church was burned. Bishop Walls was still the presiding Prelate.

> Then, followed The Reverend Swan (1972)
> The Reverend James Josey (1972-1973)
> The Reverend Rudolph Wells (1972-1995) was

reappointed to the Walls Memorial Church. Pastor Wells served faithfully and tirelessly until the LORD called him home in July 1995. Pastor Wells served a total of thirty years in pastoral ministry to this congregation and community. He served seventeen years at the St. Mark Church. He died as the active pastor of our church.

The Reverend Joseph Davis Kerr (1995-2005) who was then the Presiding Elder of the Rochester-Syracuse-Buffalo District was given the pastoral appointment following the passing of Pastor Wells. He served faithfully this charge until the LORD called him home.

The Reverend G. Michael Tydus (2005-Present) serves as our ninth pastor. During his brief time as pastor, the congregation has made significant strides. The work has been strengthened and the congregation is alive again with excitement about kingdom building. It is again making its mark in the community by opening its doors once again to support community agencies.

The ministry of Walls Memorial Church has changed over the years. The membership has changed in its configuration. However, the effectiveness of this church's witness has never waned over throughout its years. We acknowledge that if it had not been for the LORD on our side, what would we have done?

GOD's favour has been our saving grace and it is what keeps us even today.

So thanks be to kind, merciful, loving GOD who blesses us as we strive to bless Him, our Saviour, and this community as we today lift up our 59th year, before the LORD, as a congregation who works for kingdom building within the African Methodist Episcopal Zion Church body.

Submitted by Walls Memorial African Methodist Episcopal Zion Church

White Rock Missionary Baptist Church
480 East Utica Street
Buffalo, New York

The White Rock Missionary Baptist Church was organized under the leadership of Reverend Dockery in 1945 at 245 Spring Street, Buffalo, New York. Brother Johnson and Brother Singletary served as founding members of this church.

Reverend O. C. Taylor was elected pastor in 1947. He served in this position from 1947 until 1954. The White Rock Missionary Baptist Church was incorporated in 1948.

Reverend George Gayles was elected the third pastor of White Rock Missionary Baptist Church in 1954. He served in that position from 1954 to 1959. Pastor Gayles' death in August of 1959 was sudden and unexpected. Prior to Reverend Gayles' death he had relocated the church from Spring Street location to 218 Peckham Street.

In 1959, Reverend William Harrison was elected as the next Pastor of White Rock Baptist Church, and he would serve as pastor until 1962. In 1962, Pastor Harrison resigned from his position as pastor. Reverend Roosevelt Rhodes was elected in 1963 and he would serve until 1964 at which time he would resign.

The White Rock Missionary Baptist Church would be without a pastor until 1965. The Reverend James Williams was elected pastor, early in the year 1965 and would serve until 1966.

Reverend Roosevelt Williams would be elected the seventh pastor of the White Rock Missionary Baptist Church since 1945, a little over 20 years.

Deacon Ivery Daniels united with the White Rock Missionary Baptist Church in 1960 and served faithfully in that position until 1967. However, Deacon Daniels answered his call to the ministry in June 1967. In December 1967, Reverend Ivery Daniels was called and ordained as pastor of the White Rock Missionary Baptist Church. The church burned its mortgage March, 1985 eight years after acquiring it.

The early pioneers and members, of this church never lost a desire to move from a local store front ministry to a main stream ministry. In their minds, at that period of time, a larger regular church building would certainly enhance the movement. Ministry could be done with adequate space for programs, seating capacity could hold a crowd, funerals, weddings, community events could be carried out respectively. The early members of the White Rock Missionary Baptist Church sacrificed and gave the church an opportunity to do all of the above and more. The White Rock Missionary Baptist Church, under the banner and Grace of God has maintained Dr. Ivery Daniels as its pastor marching toward 45 years.

The church relocated from 218 Peckham Street to 480 East Utica Street, the current location in June 1977. This ministry has provided the White Rock Gospel Hour on WUFO 1080 from 2:00-3:00 pm on Sunday's since 1977. The church can be heard worldwide on the internet.

"To God be the Glory"

Submitted by White Rock Baptist Church

Young Tabernacle Holiness Church
623 Best Street
Buffalo, New York

Young Tabernacle Holiness Church was organized in 1954 by Reverend Lucy Hill Young as a unit of the Fire Baptized Holiness organization. The church was located in a storefront at 692 Clinton Street. Only four years after migrating to Buffalo, she had organized a new congregation and reestablished Young Tabernacle here in the city. She had founded the first Young Tabernacle in 1946 in Badham, South Carolina. In 1956, Young Tabernacle moved to 92 Monroe Street (formerly little St. John Baptist Church).In the years following, the church became known as Young Tabernacle Holiness Church of God of the Americas and severed ties with

the Fire Baptized Holiness organization. From its original six members, the church grew into an organized denominational movement with seven sister churches from northeast Ohio to central New Jersey.

By 1980, Young Tabernacle had moved to a beautiful structure at 780 William Street and Bishop Young had been elevated to the Bishopric. Young Tabernacle had a food bank, a radio and prison ministry, and several smaller missions (churches). An educational scholarship for financial support beyond high school (RAY Foundation) had been established and more than 25 ministers were promoted for gospel kingdom building. The new edifice at 623 Best Street had been purchased after a fire destroyed the William Street church. Worship services were held at 442 Pratt Street during the interim.

Under Bishop Young's leadership, deacons were ordained, trustees elevated, and over fifteen standing church auxiliaries, boards and ministries were established. These included a Ministers' Alliance and an ongoing weekly Bible study class which has continued for over three decades.

Bishop Lucy H. Young was called to her eternal rest on March 10, 1993. Reverend Marion Clay Simmons, Sr. was the next to assume the pastorate at Young Tabernacle Holiness Church. A member of the Pentecostal Holiness Church, he was a founding member of Young Tabernacle in the early 50s. He served as pastor until 2003.

Reverend Jean L. Young, a licensed, ordained gospel minister and bible study teacher, currently pastors Young Tabernacle Holiness Church and it continues to function as an independent religious entity.

Photo and history submitted by Young Tabernacle

Zion Dominion Global Ministries
895 North Forest Road
Williamsville, New York

Z ion Dominion was born in the William-Emslie YMCA with about 20 members. The congregation then rented storefront space on Sycamore Street and later on Ontario Street in Black Rock before purchasing the Genesee Street property, a building that had been slated for demolition.

In its seven years there, the congregation spent nearly $3 million renovating the building. The congregation outgrew the Genesee Street space and sought a more centralized location for its members, who hail from as far as Niagara Falls, Lockport, Rochester and the Southtowns.

 Faith, Vision, and a Historical Move: On June 12, 2005, Senior Pastor Roderick L. Hennings led Zion Dominion's family to its current fourteen acre campus at 895 North Forest Road, Amherst New York in order to accommodate a global reach. Zion Dominion previously worshipped in a 30,700 square feet cathedral at 360 Genesee Street in Buffalo. This was the first time in Western New York that people of African descent were able to purchase property of this magnitude for the purposes of worship in a predominately Caucasian suburb. Due to the growth of the membership and its outreach ministries, Zion Dominion was busting the seams at the Genesee Street edifice.

Pastor Hennings founded Zion Dominion Global Ministries in 1993. His unique ability to communicate the Word of God without compromise attracts people from different socioeconomic backgrounds, races and nationalities.

There has been a continued growth in membership from 20 at inception to currently over 5,000, the largest membership base in the Western New York area for the Church of God in Christ.

The Worship Center seats approximately 1,500 people with an overflow capacity of 400; it has plush, rose-colored carpets, cushioned pews, several television monitors and teleprompters located in the vestibule, and a motorized podium that rises with the push of a button.

The Children's wing has ten separate rooms dividing the children by age and it includes a sanctuary. The Administrative building houses 25 offices and conference room. The grounds include a pavilion, outdoor basketball court, and volleyball court. Pastor Hennings says, "Had it not been for the Lord on our side, there wouldn't be Zion Dominion Global Ministries on North Forest Road."

Over 100 children (ages 6 weeks – 12 years) enjoy weekly worship services; teens experience the joy of salvation and are given the tools for successful living through TEEN Word On Wednesdays and TNT on Saturdays; the men enjoy weekly fellowship of basketball on a regulation sized court as well as a variety of monthly activities; the women enjoy a bible study every Monday evening, Life Smart Health and Wellness program, and monthly activities of interaction. Zion Dominion ministries include We Are Manna Ministry (WAMM), Bone of My Bone Covenant Ministry, Generation Next, Children Ministry, and Abraham & Sarah Ministry. Under Pastor

Hennings leadership, Zion Dominion has become the first known church in WNY to form a little league football team under Pop Warner National Football and Cheerleading organization.

The building previously known as "Zion Dominion Church of God in Christ" was erected during the 19th century and was slated for demolition prior to its purchase by Pastor Hennings and the Zion Dominion family. The leadership of Pastor Hennings was able to minimize a $3 million debt in reconstruction to $500,000.00 in less than five years.

The city of Buffalo renamed Genesee Street "Roderick L. Hennings Way" (east to west from Jefferson Avenue to downtown). Officially ordained into the Ministry in 1982, Pastor Hennings' ministerial experience began as an Assistant Pastor in Youngstown, Ohio; an Assistant to the State Bishop of Christian's Charismatic Church (Ohio); Youth Pastor (Buffalo, NY); Pastor of True Word Holiness Church (Buffalo, NY) in 1991.

Zion Dominion is an affiliate church of the Church of God in Christ, and Pastor Hennings continues to serve the International and Jurisdictional COGIC church in several capacities. As one church with two locations, the second is at 36 East Avenue in Rochester, NY.

Zion Dominion believes in one God, omnipotent, omniscient, omnipresent, the Creator, Sustainer of the universe, revealing Himself to us in His Word as Father, Son and Holy Ghost (Spirit).

www.ziondominion.org

Zion Missionary Baptist Church
179 East Ferry Street
Buffalo, New York

*Z*ion Missionary Baptist Church was organized by our late Pastor and founder, Reverend James L. Lee, Sr. With 15 faithful members, church services and meetings were held in his home at 56 Northland Avenue. Under Pastor Lee's inspired leadership the Lord blessed the membership to grow so much that they had to move into a small storefront located at 198 East Ferry Street, Buffalo, New York (presently a part of our parking lot). Shortly thereafter, on August 27, 1950 the church was incorporated under the name of Zion Missionary Baptist Church of Buffalo, New York, Inc. Ambitious and following God's direction on April 19, 1956 we purchased a new church building located at 145-149 Maple Street, Buffalo, New York. Here, Reverend Lee labored tirelessly until he was called home by the Lord on June 26, 1962.

In the midst of their grief, God still received the Glory from the members' praise and worship, and on November 18, 1962 the Reverend R. Calvin Craven was called to Pastor Zion's sheep. With his experience and vision, Pastor Craven enabled the church to survive through financially and spiritually trying times. He was instrumental in securing a second mortgage for much needed renovations and created financial stability for Zion. He always said, "This church doesn't take in families, but individuals..."

But once again the Lord saw fit to take unto himself our beloved shepherd. Reverend R. Calvin Craven was called from labor to reward on October 5, 1971. Then in February 1972, the church called our present Pastor, Dr. Robert E. Baines, Sr., ambitious, young and eager to serve God and the Zion family, Pastor Baines came with a vision to put Zion on the list of recognition as one of Buffalo's leading Baptist churches.

Five months after his pastorate began we paid off the mortgage at 145-149 Maple Street and were able to renovate the church's parsonage. Our membership continued to grow so much that in 1975 he launched a building fund drive for the purpose of building a new church. In less than one year of fundraising, we were able to purchase a parcel of land known as 179 East Ferry Street, Buffalo, New York. By the Grace of God on Saturday August 12, 1978 at 12:00 noon we marched from Maple Street to our newly built church. As part of the ceremonies the Lord's Supper was served, candidates were baptized and babies were blessed. Pastor Baines projected a motto for the church, "A Few Plus God Equals Victory."

In August 1983, the Lord blessed us to pay off this mortgage. On October 26, 2002 the Lord showed us that he was truly in this place and well pleased by allowing we to dedicate our third newly built sanctuary at the same location. Our Pastor, Dr. Robert E. Baines, Sr. took us to unimaginable heights, and it is our hope and prayer that God will lead us even further and higher. On September 6, 2011, the Lord saw fit to take unto himself our beloved shepherd, Dr. Robert E. Baines, Sr. who was called from labor to reward after nearly forty years at Zion.

Thanks be to God for all of our pastors and all those who have labored faithfully and stayed true to the call of the Lord. We praise God for His continued blessings upon this House. God is Great, He has done Great things and He is worthy to be Praises! To God Be the Glory!

Submitted by Zion Missionary Baptist Church

WE SPEAK THEIR NAMES: A TRIBUTE TO DECEASED CLERGY

Reverend Mother Bertha Hall Amos (1903-2005) founded Pentecostal Faith Baptist Rescue Mission at 64 Steelawanna Avenue in Lackawanna, New York. Born in Moundsville, Alabama, Mother Amos moved to Lackawanna and joined Second Baptist Church. Called to the ministry in the 50's, she was led by the Holy Spirit to purchase the land on Steelawanna and build the Rescue Mission where she preached from her own pulpit. Her work as a woman of God who visited the elderly and the sick and fed the hungry was known by many in the Western New York area. (Obituary)

Bishop LeRoy Anderson (1921–2008) served as the pastor of Prince of Peace Temple of the Church of God in Christ in Buffalo and one of the 12 members of the governing body of the Church of God in Christ. Bishop Anderson's mother predicted he would follow in the footsteps of his father and preach, and in fact, he became a preacher at 16. After he moved to Buffalo, he was appointed pastor of Lackawanna Church of God in Christ and he served there until 1955, when he opened Prince of Peace Temple of the Church of God in Christ in Buffalo. In the early years, he held services out of his home. In 1963, he was appointed Bishop of Western New York Jurisdiction 1. Bishop Anderson resigned his ministry in Buffalo in 2003 and was named pastor of Emmanuel Church of God in Christ in Phoenix and Bishop of the Arizona Jurisdiction. *Buffalo News*, April 16, 2008

Reverend Samuel Austin (1935-1998) was only nineteen years old when he became pastor of Buffalo's Pilgrim Baptist Church in 1955 and he served in that position for seven years. A native of Montgomery, Alabama, Reverend Austin came to Buffalo as a child and delivered his first sermon at age twelve and was educated in the city's public schools. In 1964, Reverend Austin became pastor of Grace Baptist Church in Mount Vernon. For 24 years, Reverend Austin served as pastor of the 3,000-member Brown Memorial Baptist Church in Brooklyn. In addition, he had served as president of the Empire State Missionary Baptist Convention. *Buffalo News*, February 4, 1998

Reverend Robert E. Baines, Sr. (1947-2011) served as pastor of Zion Missionary Baptist Church, where he celebrated his 40th anniversary. Born in Skipper, Virginia, he relocated to Buffalo in 1960 with his family. He became pastor of Antioch Fire Baptized Holiness Church in the late 1960's. In 2003, he received an honorary of Doctor of Divinity degree from Houghton College. Reverend Baines also was a chaplain with the Buffalo Police Department for over a decade. *Buffalo News*, September 11, 2011

Reverend Arsell Bell (1928-2007) served as pastor of State Tabernacle Church of God in Christ from 1953--2007. Reverend Bell was born in Starkville, Mississippi, and moved to Buffalo in 1944. He started out in 1954 as a deacon at State Tabernacle, which was founded by his late uncle and aunt, Elder Robert and Mother Charlotte Brown, before he was ordained a minister and later became pastor of the church. Reverend Bell also served as superintendent of the 9th District of the First Ecclesiastical Jurisdiction of Western New York of the Churches of God in Christ for more than 35 years. *Buffalo News*, December 1, 2007

Reverend L. T. Boyce (1916-1991) served as the pastor of Calvary Baptist for 28 years. He entered the ministry in 1954 after serving eighteen years as a deacon. Born in Memphis, Tennessee, he had served at churches in Mississippi and Tennessee. In Buffalo, Reverend Boyce was instrumental in moving Calvary from 539 William Street to 1184 Genesee Street in 1972. Three years later in 1975, he and the congregation celebrated payment of the church's mortgage seven years earlier than expected. He was a past president of the Baptist Ministers Conference of Buffalo, past first vice president of the Empire State Baptist Congress of Christian Education and an instructor of the National Baptist Convention U.S.A. Inc. Reverend Boyce was a board member of the Council of Churches of Buffalo; the Baptist Bible School of Western New York, and the Inter-denominational Ministers' Alliance of Western New York. *Buffalo News*, July 16, 1991

Reverend Maggie Y. Boyd (1948-2005) served as pastor of Metropolitan United Methodist Church from 1997 until 2005. Born in Chester, South Carolina, she answered the call to ministry in 1978 in Rock Hill, South Carolina. She completed her degree at Colgate Rochester Divinity School. In 1985, Reverend Boyd was ordained by the Christian Methodist Episcopal Church. She started the Graves Institutional CME Church in Rochester, New York and served as the pastor there from 1984-1992. *Obituary*

Reverend William V. Callahan Jr. (1952-1992) served as an associate minister of the Trinity Baptist Church. Born in Buffalo, he was active in Trinity as a youth. He entered the ministry in 1974. After five years at Trinity, he was appointed assistant pastor of Macedonia Baptist Church in Albany in 1979, and he remained for six years. Reverend Callahan then served as the pastor of Riverview Missionary Baptist Church. *Buffalo News*, October 24, 1992

Reverend Kenneth S. Curry (1925-1990) served as the Rector of St. Phillips Episcopal Church for seventeen years. Born in Canton, Ohio, he was ordained to the Episcopal priesthood in the Diocese of Chicago. In 1958, Reverend Curry established the St. Philip's Community Center. He also served as chaplain at the former Emergency Hospital (Sheehan).*Buffalo News*, March 4, 1990

Reverend Joseph Davis (1918-2008) served as pastor of Masten Park United Methodist Church and later Trinity Baptist Church. Born in Kansas City, Kansas, Reverend Davis moved to Buffalo as a teenager. He served his pastoral internship at Humboldt Parkway Baptist Church under Pastor W. Phillips. Reverend Davis also served as a chaplain at the Veteran's Hospital. *Buffalo News*, July 8, 2008

Reverend William Davis (1917-2001) was the founding pastor of Mount Zion Church of God in Christ. Born in Rome, Georgia, Reverend Davis founded Mount Zion Church in the early 1970s and served as its pastor until his retirement in 1994. A minister for more than 40 years, Reverend Davis also served as superintendent of the denomination's District 14. *Buffalo News,* May 11, 2001

Reverend Elroy L. Day Sr. (1923-2005) former pastor of Tabernacle Baptist Church headed the Buffalo congregation for 27 years. Born in Greenville, Mississippi, he graduated from Natchez Theological Seminary. Reverend Day headed churches in Leavenworth, Kansas, Shreveport, Louisiana, and Los Angeles before coming to Buffalo in 1967. Before stepping down as pastor of Tabernacle Baptist in 1994, he guided the congregation's move from its building on Johnson Street to a vacant church at Northland Avenue and Humboldt Parkway. *Buffalo News,* February 25, 2005

Reverend Fannie Mae Dozier (1926-2002) served as pastor of Mount Calvary Prayer Room at 643 William Street. Born in Kingstree, South Carolina, she moved to Buffalo in 1946. Ordained in 1960 in Mount Calvary Holiness Church of America, she later opened the first of a series of storefront churches. Reverend Dozier had served as a minister in Mount Calvary Holiness Church of America and as assistant pastor of Loral Swamp Missionary Baptist Church, Salters, South Carolina. *Buffalo News,* September 25, 2002

Reverend Glenn H. DuBois (1920-2005) served as pastor of Jordan Grove Baptist Church. Born and raised in Knoldon, Arkansas, Reverend DuBois moved to Buffalo in 1951. Before becoming pastor at Jordan Grove Baptist Church in 1964, he attended Buffalo Bible Institute. Reverend DuBois was a member of the Baptist Ministers Conference, Great Lakes Baptist Association, Empire State Baptist Convention, and the National Baptist Convention. *Buffalo News,* February 14, 2005

Reverend Elijah J. Echols, Sr. (1878-1961) served for 43 years as pastor of First Shiloh from 1918 until 1961. In November 1918, the congregation called him and he accepted.

He was born in Columbus, Mississippi. In May 1921, the church congregation moved into the building at 40 Cedar Street. For the next forty-five years, this building was the home of the First Shiloh Baptist Church. *Obituary*

Reverend Elijah Echols, Jr. (1914-1984) was elected to succeed his father as pastor of First Shiloh. Born in Starksville, Mississippi, he moved to Buffalo as a child. In 1943, he was ordained into the ministry under Reverend Echols, Sr. In March 1962, he was installed and he remained the pastor for 22 years. As pastor, he presided over the construction of the new church building at 15 Pine Street which began as a dream of his father. Reverend Echols served as President of the Board of Directors of the Buffalo Area Council of Churches, and President of the Empire State Baptist Convention. *Obituary*

Reverend Henry Ford (1925-1987) founded Jordan Grove Baptist Church in 1955. Born in Hughes, Arkansas, Reverend Ford pastored Jordan Grove until 1964. He also pastored the St. Mark Baptist Church in Long Beach, California. *Obituary*

Reverend Clarence L. Franklin (1915 -1984) served for two years as the pastor of Friendship Baptist Church at 146 Hickory Street. Reverend Franklin moved to Buffalo from Memphis in 1944 following the death of the former pastor, Reverend Jennings. Along with the Friendship Baptist United Choir, Reverend Franklin gave performances in Kleinhans Music Hall, and the music, along with the Reverend Franklin's preaching, were broadcast on WKBW Radio. *Buffalo News*, June 4, 1991

Reverend Maceo M. Freeman (1939- 2003) served as pastor of Centennial African Methodist Episcopal Zion Methodist at 127 Doat Street from 1979-2003 and was well known in the community for his efforts to rid the neighborhood of crime and for starting a soup kitchen that has served thousands of meals. Reverend Freeman worked for many years as a chaplain in the New York State prison system at Collins, Albion and Wyoming County Correctional Facilities. A native of Delco, N.C., he was called to the ministry in 1966. He was pastor of three churches in the Cape Fear Conference of the African Methodist Episcopal Zion Church in North Carolina prior to his transfer to Buffalo in 1974. He also served as pastor of Durham Memorial African Methodist Episcopal Zion Church from 1974 to 1979. *Buffalo News,* October 8, 2003

Reverend Henry Hall (1893-1993) began his ministry preaching on Buffalo street corners. A native of Frazier, Tennessee, he moved to Buffalo and was about 20 years old, when suddenly, he got a calling to do the Lord's work. In 1918, he joined Shiloh Baptist Church. Reverend Hall preached on street corners for about 12 years before local churches invited him to be a guest preacher. Standing on a little platform that he carried with him and wearing a black robe, he would appear outside a tavern and begin singing "Wade in the Water, Children." Reverend Hall was pastor of Jefferson Avenue Community Church from 1959 to 1960. A member of Antioch Baptist Church since 1989, he preached his last sermon there on Easter Sunday in 1992. Known as a "fiery evangelist," he also served as superintendent of evangelism of the Great Lakes Baptist Association and founded the Upper Room Prayer Band, which made annual New Year's Day visits to the Erie County Home and Infirmary to provide gifts. He gained evangelical renown following the example of the itinerant black ministers of the Old South. *Buffalo News* - Sunday, April 11, 1993; Saturday, June 17, 1989

Reverend Nathan S. Halton (1953-2006) established the Greater Faith Bible Tabernacle Church, Inc. After he moved his family from Cleveland, Ohio to Buffalo, New York in December 1981, Reverend Halton opened the doors of his home for prayer and bible studies. After several months of fellowship and demonstrative presence of the Lord's favor Greater Faith Bible Tabernacle was founded. The ministry grew along with the needs of the community and through the sagacious leadership of the Lord's anointed other ministries were birthed, including The Breath of Life Ministries, Inc.,

Breath of Life Media, Breath of Life Day Care, and Educational Center, and the Greater Faith Housing Corporation. <http://www.faithbibletab.com/>

Reverend James T. Hemphill Sr. (1929-2002) founded and served as pastor of Hemphill Interdenominational Church early in his ministry in Buffalo. Beginning in 1958, he served for many years as pastor of Walls Memorial African Methodist Episcopal Zion Church, where he organized a recreation and athletic club that served up to 600 youngsters. Reverend Hemphill retired in 1998 as pastor of Varick Metropolitan African Methodist Episcopal Zion Church. In addition to serving Buffalo churches, he was a pastor of churches in North and South Carolina and Alabama. *Buffalo News*, May 16, 2002

Reverend William R. Holley, Jr. (1935- 2005) was the founder and pastor of St. James Missionary Baptist Church where he served for 33 years. A native of Gadsden, Alabama, he was ordained and licensed at Jordan Grove Missionary Baptist Church pastored by the late Reverend Henry Ford and later the late Reverend Glenn DuBois. Reverend Holley also pastored the Community Missionary Baptist Church. He belonged to the Western New York Baptist Ministers Conference. *Obituary*

Reverend O. Urcille Ifill Sr. (1921-1991) former pastor of Delaine Waring African Methodist Episcopal Church. As the third pastor of Delaine Waring Church, Reverend Ifill served for two years in the early 1960s. Reverend Ifill was also a co-founder of the African Methodist Episcopal Ministers' Alliance here. *Buffalo News*, December 3, 1991

Reverend W.L. Jones (1931-1992) founded and organized the Mt. Ararat Baptist Church at 603 Clinton Street. In 1965, the church moved to 971 Jefferson Avenue. Reverend Jones was born in Lake Providence, Louisiana. In 1953 he moved to

Buffalo and joined the Open Door Church of God in Christ where he was called into the ministry. Reverend Jones had the vision of senior housing which was realized in the construction of God's City. *Obituary*

Reverend Joseph D. Kerr (1925-2005) served as pastor of Walls Memorial African Methodist Episcopal Zion Church from 1995-2005. Born in Atlantic City, New Jersey, Reverend Kerr earned a bachelor's degree in divinity from Interdenominational Theological Seminary in Atlanta. In the early 1990s, he settled in Buffalo. In the 1970s, Reverend Kerr moved to upstate New York and served as presiding elder of the AME Zion Church in Western New York and as pastor of several African Methodist Episcopal Zion churches in Jamestown, Syracuse, and Rochester. *Buffalo News*, December 12, 2005

Reverend Nathaniel A. Mason (1898-1962) was called to pastor New Hope Missionary Baptist Church in August 1928. The building at 63 Union Street was erected in 1932, and he moved his congregation to the edifice at 543 Richmond Avenue in 1960. Reverend Mason was a member of the Empire State Baptist Convention, National Baptist Convention, Great Lakes District Baptist Association, and the Baptist Minister's Conference. *Obituary*

Reverend Landen L. McCall Sr. (1921-2006) served as the pastor of People's Community Church and True Christian African Methodist Episcopal Zion in Rochester. Born in Manning, South Carolina, the late Reverends McCarley and Austin of the Empire Baptist Church Association performed his ordination. He began as a member of the Buffalo clergy in 1974 when he was appointed as assistant pastor of St. Luke African Methodist Episcopal Zion Church. A barber by trade for over forty years, Reverend McCall served generations of Buffalo families. *Obituary*

Reverend Burnie C. McCarley (1894-1972) was the founding pastor of St. John Baptist Church. Born in Camden, South Carolina, he arrived in Buffalo in 1924 and was ordained by Reverend John Crockett at Pleasant Grove. Reverend McCarley opened the doors of St. John with four members in a storefront in 1927. He continued as pastor until 1972. Pastor McCarley was a member of Empire State Baptist Convention, National Baptist Convention, and the Baptist Ministers Alliance. *Obituary*

Bishop Charles Henry McCoy (1905-1996) served as pastor of Pentecostal Temple Church of God in Christ at 618 Jefferson Avenue. He had served as Bishop of the denomination's Second Western New York Jurisdiction since 1969. Bishop McCoy is best known for building the C.H. McCoy Convention Center at 653 Clinton Street. The son of a Baptist minister, Bishop McCoy was born in Sumter, South Carolina. He moved to Buffalo when he was 12. In 1925, he became assistant pastor to Elder B.E. Reid at Saints Home Church of God in Christ. Ordained in 1935, Bishop McCoy also served the Church of God in Christ as district superintendent and a pastor in Rochester and Olean. *Buffalo News*, September 27, 1996

Reverend Edward D. McNeely (1910-1977) was called to pastor Friendship Baptist Church in 1948, and he served for twenty-nine years. Born in Clinton, Arkansas, he embarked upon his mission in the ministry in his teens. Before arriving in Buffalo, Reverend McNeely pastored churches in Arkansas, Mississippi, Tennessee, and Illinois. He held office in the Empire State Missionary Baptist Convention, Western District Baptist Association, and was a member of the Baptist Ministers Conference and the Interdenominational Ministers Council. Reverend McNeely, along with other local ministers, was influential in bringing the 94th Annual National Baptist Convention USA, Inc. to Buffalo in 1974. *Obituary*

Reverend Joseph W. Moore (1918-1976) served as pastor of the New Hope Baptist Church for over twelve years. Born in

Camden, South Carolina, Reverend Moore served churches in Pennsylvania, New Jersey, Michigan and New York for over 29 years. He served as president of the Baptist Ministers Conference, and member of the American Baptist State Convention and the Black American Baptist Caucus of New York. *Obituary*

Reverend J. Edward Nash (1868-1957) served as the pastor of Michigan Avenue Baptist Church for 61 years from 1892 until his retirement in 1953. Born in Occoquam, Virginia, the son of slave parents, Reverend Nash graduated from Whalen Seminary (Virginia Union University). Reverend Adam Clayton Powell, Sr. pastor of Harlem's Abyssinian Baptist Church was close friend and former college classmate. In 1910 he was host to Booker T. Washington during Washington's meeting with "Afro-American Citizens of Buffalo."He was instrumental in founding the Buffalo Urban League and the local branch of the N.A.A.C.P. In 1953, Potter Street was renamed Nash Street in his honor. He was a long-time leader and treasurer of the Western New York Baptist Association. For 32 years he was secretary of the Ministers Alliance of Buffalo. *Obituary*, < *http://www.nashhousemuseum.org*>

Reverend Annie C. Hargrave Pinn (1931-2005) pastor of Mount Zion African Methodist Episcopal Church for 10 years. Born in Lackawanna, Reverend Pinn accepted Jesus Christ and was baptized in 1944. She entered the ministry at Agape African Methodist Episcopal Church. Reverend Pinn was ordained a local deacon by Bishop Hilderbrand and a local elder by Bishop Cummings. She was the first woman elected president of the African Methodist Ministers Alliance. *Obituary*

Reverend Herbert V. Reid, (1936-2008) was the pastor of Gethsemane Missionary Baptist Church at 55 Grape Street for 45 years and a leader in the community's civil rights movement. Born in Sanford, Florida, he was studying at Rochester's Colgate Divinity School when in 1962, by chance, Reverend Reid was invited at age 20 to be a guest preacher at

Gethsemane. Reverend Reid returned to Gethsemane after completing his studies and saw it grow into one of the largest and better-known Baptist congregations in the area. He held the position of president of the Empire State Baptist Congress of Christian Education. Reverend Reid was also senior chaplain at the Erie County Holding Center. *Buffalo News,* December 1, 2008

Bishop Carl Roberson Sr. (1919-2010) served as pastor of Saints Home Church of God in Christ and Prayer Room Church of God in Christ in Batavia, New York. Born in Texas, Bishop Roberson moved to Buffalo in 1953. He was the Past Prelate of Alaska and South Dakota. *Buffalo News,* May 16, 2010

Elder Edward Sanders (1926-1990) was ordained as pastor of the Open Door #1 Church of God in Christ in 1973 by Presiding Prelate Bishop C.H. McCoy of Jurisdiction #2. Born in Prattville, Alabama, he moved to Buffalo in 1951. He was saved and filled with the Holy Spirit under the leadership of the late Elder Peter P. Mann in 1954.

Reverend Willie B. Seals (1910-1995) served as pastor of Cold Spring Baptist Church in the late 1950s. Born in Alexandria, Louisiana, he was called to the ministry at an early age. He pastored his first church at age 23 and several in Alexandria before moving to Buffalo. Reverend Seals joined St. John Baptist Church in 1946 and served as an assistant and associate pastor. He also served as interim pastor of the New Hope Baptist Church in Niagara Falls, New York. An accomplished musician, he founded the Bells of St. John and later became a well-known photographer. *Obituary*

Reverend Marion Clay Simmons, Sr. served as pastor of Young Tabernacle Holiness Church from 1993-2003. Born in Charleston, South Carolina, he came to Buffalo in 1951. A member of the Pentecostal Holiness Church, Reverend Simmons was a founding member of Young Tabernacle Holiness Church in the early 1950s. He had served as brother, trustee and deacon before being licensed in 1964 and ordained in 1970; Reverend Simmons became assistant pastor in the early 1970s. *Buffalo News,* October 25, 2003

Reverend Augustus Smith (1927-2005) a Baptist minister and founder of Peace Baptist Church, was a native of Calhoun Falls, S.C. He moved to Buffalo in 1944. He was a self-employed barber for about 30 years and owned a shop on William Street. In 1959, he was called to Baptist ministry and served at Friendship Baptist Church for about a year. Reverend Smith formed Peace Baptist Church in 1960 and was pastor for 44 years. He continued his affiliation with Friendship Baptist Church, where he served on the board of deacons.. A member of the Baptist Ministers Conference of Buffalo and Vicinity, Reverend Smith loved preaching the word of God. *Buffalo News,* January 6, 2005

Reverend Bennett W. Smith, Sr. (1933-2001) was called to become the second pastor of St. John Baptist Church in 1972. Born in Florence, Alabama, he was ordained during the pastorate of Reverend Vencheal Booth at Zion Baptist Church in Cincinnati, Ohio. There he pastored First Baptist Church and Lincoln Heights. As pastor of St. John for 29 years, the civil rights leader who marched with the Reverend Martin Luther King Jr. from Selma to Montgomery, served as President of the Progressive National Baptist Convention, Inc. and brought the Convention to Buffalo in 1997. Reverend Smith was a member of the Baptist Ministers Conference of Buffalo and Vicinity, World Council of Churches, Congress of National Black Churches and a leader of the Religious Action Network of the American Committee on Africa. *Buffalo News,* August 9, 2001

Reverend Coleman Spate (1929-2000) served as pastor of the Harriet Tubman AME Church in Niagara Falls, New York. He answered the call to ministry in 1977. Born in Jakin, Georgia, he joined the St. Luke African Methodist Episcopal Zion Church after moving to Buffalo. *Obituary*

Reverend Richard G. Stewart (1940-2010) was assigned to pastor Durham Memorial AME Church in 1990, and he served until he retired in 2009. Durham Memorial, on East Eagle Street, was his childhood church. He began his pastoral career while a student at Hood Theological Seminary. Reverend Stewart pastored Walls AME Zion Church from 1981-1989 after serving as pastor of churches in North Carolina, Texas and Michigan. *Obituary*

Reverend Samuel B. Sutton, (1906-1999) served for 23 years as senior pastor of Second Temple Missionary Baptist Church. A minister for 53 years, he retired in 1990. Born in Lily, Georgia, he earlier had served for eight years as pastor of Mount Olive Baptist Church, Lackawanna. Before becoming pastor of the Buffalo church, he spent 20 years as pastor of Riverview Baptist Church near Albany. Reverend Sutton had served as vice president of the Empire State Missionary Baptist Convention, and a member of the board of the Social Commission of the National Baptist Convention USA. As a pastor, Reverend Sutton was widely known as "Reverend Stewardship" because of his continuing efforts to promote stewardship as a way of life, recognizing God as the owner of everything. *Buffalo News*, July 1, 1999

Reverend Osborn M. Taylor (1927-1992) served as pastor of Greater St. Matthew Baptist Church at 450 William Street for more than twenty years, after its organization in 1983. Born in Northumberland County, North Carolina, Reverend Taylor was ordained as a minister at Pilgrim Baptist Church. *Buffalo News*, June 10, 1992

Reverend Precious Charles Lindbergh Thompson (1927-2010) served as pastor of Jerusalem Missionary Baptist Church at 465 Glenwood Avenue for 50 years. Born in McCool, Mississippi, he began honing his preaching talents early. According to his family, Reverend Thompson, as a young child, used to offer his sermons to the farm animals that surrounded him, particularly the chickens. He moved to Buffalo as a young adult and joined Calvary Baptist Church, then located on Spring Street. He attended the Buffalo Bible Institute, where he received his ordination and in 1957 was appointed pastor of Mount Calvary Baptist Church on Masten Avenue. The church was later renamed Jerusalem Missionary Baptist Church. *Buffalo News*, January 8, 2010

Reverend Dr. Paul F. **Thompson** (1933--2008) served as pastor of New Hope Baptist Church from 1980--2000. Dr. Thompson was born and attended school in Kinston, North Carolina. Ordained in 1959, he began his ministry as an assistant to the pastor at Antioch Baptist Church in 1959. He served as pastor at Emmanuel Baptist Church in Niagara Falls from 1961—1964, and he also served as part-time chaplain at the Veterans Administration Medical Center in Buffalo from 1984--1994. After his retirement from New Hope Baptist Church, Dr. Thompson served as minister of seniors at the Friendship Missionary Baptist Church in Charlotte, N.C., from 2001 to 2003. And in 2005 and 2006, he was the interim pastor at Delaware Avenue Baptist Church in Buffalo. For 26 years, he served as the national secretary of the Black American Baptist Caucus. *Buffalo News,* August 25, 2008

Reverend Peter Trammell (1895-1962) served as the pastor of [Mount] Calvary Baptist Church for 24 years. A native of Lafayette, Alabama, he was installed in 1938. At Calvary, he established the first Deacon and Trustee Boards along with the church school. Reverend Trammell installed and ordained pastors at Jordan Grove and True Bethel Baptist Church. www.calvarybaptistchurch.org

Reverend A. Charles Ware (1927-1998) served for 20 years as pastor of Friendship Missionary Baptist Church, 402 Clinton Street. Born in Macon, Mississippi, the son of a share-cropper, Reverend Ware, grew up in the cotton fields and became a Baptist minister in 1958 in Memphis, Tennessee. Before coming to Buffalo, Reverend Ware served as pastor of Eastern Star Missionary Baptist Church in Toledo, Ohio and others in

Mississippi, Arkansas and Tennessee. Reverend Ware was moderator of the Western District Baptist Association, a member of the executive board of the evangelistic board of the National Baptist Convention USA, chairman of the board of the Empire State Missionary Baptist Convention of New York and a state representative for the board of evangelism for the same organization. *Obituary*

Reverend Whitfield Washington Jr. (1943-2007) served as pastor of First Calvary Missionary at 467 William Street for 34 years. Born in Ida Mae, West Virginia, he moved to Buffalo in the early 1950s. He preached his first sermon in 1961 and was ordained as a Baptist minister in 1963. He attended the Buffalo Bible College and was a graduate of Missouri Valley College in Marshall, Missouri where he started his pastoral ministry. He served as president of Great Lakes District, Buffalo Baptist Ministers Conference; and vice president of Area Two, Empire State Convention. *Buffalo News*, April 26, 2007

Reverend Rudolph L. Wells (1920's-1995) was the founder of Walls Memorial African Methodist Episcopal Zion Church in 1946, formerly Trinity African Methodist Episcopal Zion Church. Born in Birmingham, Alabama, he moved to Buffalo in the early 1940s. Reverend Wells was pastor for ten years before being assigned to St. Mark's African Methodist Episcopal Zion Church in Lackawanna. In 1973, Reverend Wells returned to Walls Memorial, where he remained pastor until his death. *Buffalo News*, July 11, 1995

Reverend Reginald Whatley (1920-1999) was pastor of St. Mark's in Lackawanna and served as an associate pastor of Walls Memorial African Methodist Episcopal Zion Church in Buffalo. He later became assistant pastor of St. Luke's African Methodist Episcopal Zion Church in Buffalo. A native of Gaston, Alabama, Reverend Whatley became an ordained minister in 1974. In the early 1940s, he moved from Alabama to Lackawanna and became a member of St. Mark's African Methodist Episcopal Zion Church. Later, Reverend Whatley became a member and associate pastor of New Hope Baptist Church. *Buffalo News*, February 3, 1999

Bishop Milton A. Williams Sr. (1938–2005) served as pastor of Durham Memorial A.M.E. Zion Church from 1965 until 1970. Born in Mocksville, North Carolina, he was a member of the African Methodist Episcopal Zion Church from birth. He graduated from Livingstone College and earned a master of divinity degree from Hood Theological Seminary. Bishop Williams founded Shaw Memorial A.M.E. Zion Church in 1970 and served as its pastor until 1981. While in Buffalo, he was presiding elder of the Rochester-Syracuse-Buffalo District of the A.M.E. Zion Church and later served as prelate of the 12th Episcopal District. Residing in Belleville, Illinois, he was presiding bishop of the Mid-West Episcopal District. *Buffalo News*, December 9, 2005

Reverend Samuel W. Williams Jr. (1928-1991) served as pastor of New Zion Institutional Missionary Baptist Church, 318 High Street. A native of Holly Grove, Arkansas, he was the son and grandson of Baptist ministers, and he toured extensively as a gospel singer before being ordained in 1946. He came to New Zion Baptist Church in Buffalo in 1969. His pastoral service includes 45 years at six churches in four states. *Buffalo News*, February 27, 1991

Reverend J. B. Williamson (1904-1989) was the founder and pastor of Triedstone Baptist Church in 1944. Born in Pell City, Alabama, Reverend Williamson was called into the ministry at an early age. Upon his arrival in Buffalo, he pastored First Baptist Church in Lackawanna. Reverend Williamson was a member of the Baptist Ministers' Conference of Buffalo and the Empire State Baptist Convention. *Obituary*

Elder Adolph Young (1928-1994) served as pastor of Lackawanna Church of God in Christ. Born in Birmingham, Alabama into of a family of ministers, he had been pastor of the Lackawanna church for four years. Previously, he had served for 17 years as pastor of God's Temple Church of God in Christ at 814 Broadway, and he had held various offices in the Church of God in Christ. Buffalo News, June 2, 1994

Bishop Lucy H. Young (1918-1993) was the founder and religious leader of Young Tabernacle Holiness Church. Born in Dorchester, South Carolina, she came to Buffalo in 1950. She had received the divine call to ministry in 1949.Reverend Young and her late husband, Wilson H. Young founded Young Tabernacle Church at 692 Clinton Street, making it a unit of the FBH under Bishop W.E. Fuller. The church was renamed Young Tabernacle Holiness Church of God of the Americas and she was ordained to the bishopric in 1980. *Buffalo News*, March 14, 1993; Biography of Bishop Young submitted by Pastor Jean Young

HOUSES OF WORSHIP HISTORIANS

Sharon R. Amos, Fern E. Beavers........St. John Baptist Church

Reva Betha........................Lutheran Church of Our Savior

Florence Hargrave Curtis..................Mt. Zion AME Church

Lurie DuBois.......................Jordan Grove Baptist Church

Monroe Fordham...............Michigan Avenue Baptist Church

Priscilla Hill Parker................New Covenant United Church

Terry Patterson............................Agape AME Church

Sharon A. Savannah.................New Hope Baptist Church

LaVita Spence.............Enter In Full Gospel Baptist Church

Richard Stewart (deceased).........Durham AME Zion Church

Bernice Wiggins............................Trinity Baptist Church

Lillian S. Williams.......................Mt. Zion Baptist Church
NiagaraFalls, NY

SOURCES

Buffalo News Obituaries <http://infoweb.newsbank.com>

Fordham, Monroe. African American History of Forest Lawn
Cemetery <http://www.monroefordham.org> August 7,
2011.

Goldman, Mark. *High Hopes*. Albany: SUNY Press, 1983.

Hargrave Curtis, Florence, ed. *Taking the Old Path and Preserving
Our Legacy: A Historical View of the Churches in the Western New
York African Methodist Episcopal Conference*, 2007.

"Historic Michigan Street Baptist Church founded on the
Strength of Unity Driven on Hope for 163 Years."
<http://www.themichiganstreetbaptistchurch.org>

Salvatore, Nick. *Singing in a Strange Land: C.L. Franklin, the Black
Church, and the Transformation of America*. New York: Little and
Brown Company 2006.

Simmons, Martha and Frank A. Thomas, eds. *Preaching with
Sacred Fire: An Anthology of African American Sermons, 1750 to the
Present*. New York: W.W. Norton &Company Inc., 2010.

Stewart, Richard. "Durham Memorial A.M.E. Zion Church:
Making the Dream a Reality." *New York Landmarks Conservancy
Common Bond* Vol. 10, No.1, April 1994
<http://www.sacredplaces.org>

Williams, Lillian Serece. *Strangers in the Land of Paradise*.
Bloomington: Indiana Press, 1999.

About the Editors of Open Doors: WNYAAHW

Sharon R. Amos Ph.D is one of the church historians at St. John Baptist Church. Committed to documenting and preserving the rich history of our religious institutions, she is the co-producer of the video, *Yielding to the Spirit: A History of St. John Baptist Church*. Additionally, she is the president of the Buffalo Genealogical Society of the African Diaspora (BGSAD) and a member of the Afro-American Historical Association. A graduate of Canisius and the University at Buffalo, Sharon joined St. John in 1966, and has served on church's Historical Gallery Committee since 1990. In the early 1900's, her great great grandfather, Robert Richardson (1835-1920), was a founding member of the family church, Rose Hill Baptist which began under a brush arbor in Lancaster, South Carolina.

Sharon A. Savannah has a degree in sociology from Canisius College and is the church historian at New Hope Baptist Church. She joined New Hope in 1964 and has served as historian since 2000. She is committed to the documenting and preservation of the rich history of our religious institutions. Sharon is also a member of the Buffalo Genealogical Society of the African Diaspora (BGSAD), and is a founding partner of the Acting in Faith Theater Company, Buffalo, New York.

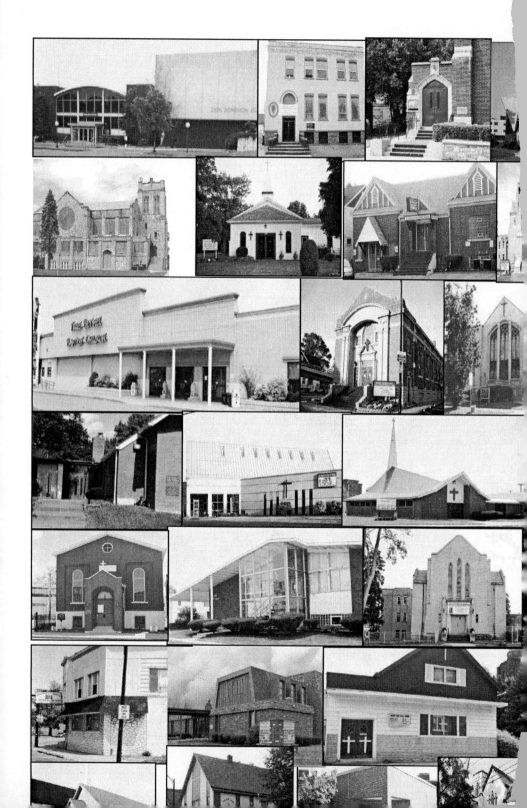